ON MANAGING

MARK H. McCORMACK ON MANAGING

ISBN: 0-7871- 1564-9

NewStar Press
a division of NewStar Media Inc.
8955 Beverly Boulevard
Los Angeles, CA 90048

Cover design by Rick Penn-Kraus
Text design and layout by Frank Loose Design
Printed by Wright Color Graphics

First NewStar Trade Paperback Printing: October 1998

10 9 8 7 6 5 4 3 2 1

Contents

CHAPTER 10

There Are No Buzzwords Here

I am not a management guru, at least not in the sense that I have an all-encompassing theory that will cure whatever ails an organization. If anything, I'm a management antiguru. A part of my brain shuts down when I hear gurulike buzzwords such as "paradigm" and "re-engineering" and "empowerment."

It's not that I don't think these buzzwords have any application in the real world. They do have value—but only if you remember that any buzzword, no matter how clever or attractive, must eventually run through that unpredictable filter known as people. A management concept is meaningless without a shrewd understanding of people.

For example, "leadership" was the management phrase on everyone's lips a few short years ago. The ideal manager had to be a strong omniscient leader who, by sheer Churchillian force of will and personality, could make people yield to his or her vision.

Not long thereafter, "leadership" was transmuted into "empowerment." Suddenly managers had to do more than lead. They had to be able to turn the people below them into the same strong leaders. They accomplished this by empowering them with more and more authority. In doing so, they were developing good managers and building a strong corporate infrastructure.

It's hard to argue with this, of course. The value of developing good managers is self-evident. What tickles me, though, is the notion that "empowerment" is something new. In truth, empowerment is just a fancy word for delegating. And delegating is the essence of management.

But my big problem with buzzwords is that they willfully ignore the human element in most management situations. Coining a new phrase to describe what managers do is just clever repackaging. The new package may attract people, but packaging alone won't hold their attention. There will always be another "new and improved" package that will capture their fancy. The concepts that last don't rely on a nifty turn of phrase. They rely on an understanding of people.

When it comes to the concept of empowerment, you don't have to look too far to see how human nature—that is, the people factor—can confound an activity that should be simple to do. Of all the reasons bosses don't empower their subordinates, nearly all boil down to ego.

I remember meeting with a European broadcasting CEO not long ago. Accompanying this sixty-year-old CEO was a gentleman about twenty years his junior whom the CEO introduced as his "number two man." The CEO was obviously grooming this associate because he spent several minutes describing how bright the fellow was and how hard he had worked to lure him away from a competitor. I had to take the CEO's word about his number two's brilliance, because there was no evidence of it in our meeting. The CEO didn't let him say a word other than "hello" and "good-bye."

I left that meeting wondering why he bothered to bring the young man at all. What would it have cost the CEO to just sit back and let his heir apparent do all the talking? It would have given the younger man experience. It would have increased his stature and credibility in my eyes. Most important, it would make the CEO more effective. Having teed up his number two with me, he might not have to attend future meetings with us and would be free to pursue opportunities elsewhere. That would have been a form of empowerment. Incredibly simple, incredibly effective. But his ego stood in the way.

I feel obliged to mention all this at the start as a form of truth in advertising. It's my official warning to readers. If you're looking for the latest slickly packaged concepts, freshly minted by globe-trotting consultants or silver-tongued professors from American business schools, you won't find them here.

What you will find instead is my hard-won advice on what I consider the root activities of a manager—establishing his or her authority, making smart decisions, hiring (and keeping) good employees, controlling costs, anticipating and dealing with crises, running effective meetings, and maintaining growth.

At this point, you should be asking who I am to teach and preach on managing.

My only credential is that I run a sports marketing company, which I started thirty-five years ago in Cleveland, Ohio, with $500 in capital, called International Management Group, or simply IMG.

We represent hundreds of well-known athletes such as Arnold Palmer (my first client), Jackie Stewart, Jean-Claude Killy, Bjorn Borg, Martina Navratilova, Alberto Tomba, and Andre Agassi. In recent years, we have branched out into the representation of classical musicians and singers such as Itzhak Perlman, James Galway, and Sir Neville Marriner.

We create and manage events, everything from the Toyota World Match Play at Wentworth to a Jose Carreras concert in Singapore to the Detroit Grand Prix motor race to *Jesus Christ Superstar* in Sydney to the Dubai Snooker Classic.

We represent the Nobel Foundation. We have helped develop the commercial interests of Wimbledon and the Royal and Ancient Golf Club of St. Andrews.

Our television arm, Trans World International, has represented the international broadcast rights for sports properties such as the Olympic Games, the World and European Figure Skating championships, the National Football League, all the major golf and tennis championships, and the 24 Hours of Le Mans. It is also the world's largest independent producer of television sports programming.

Although I started out as a lawyer at a large established law firm with no management skills to speak of, I realized quickly when I went out on my own that, if I wanted to stay in business, I would have to start thinking about how I run my business.

In 1984 when I wrote my first book, *What They Don't Teach You at Harvard Business School*, IMG had 500 employees in nineteen offices around the world generating several hundred million dollars in revenue. Today, we have 2000 employees and seventy-three offices in twenty-eight countries, and revenues have surged well beyond the billion-dollar mark.

In the interval, I feel I have faced many of the same situations that challenge (if not befuddle) every other manager.

As a result, the managing examples you'll read here are personal. They have all involved me or our company in some way. In other words, they're real. In some cases I look brilliant, in others not so brilliant. I cite the triumphs and disasters with equal liberalness so you can emulate the former and not repeat the latter.

My only caveat (and I have said this as well of the two previous volumes in this series, *On Negotiating* and *On Selling*) is that this management primer has a beginning, middle, and end. I've sometimes described my earlier books as "popcorn." Like a bag of popcorn, you can dip in anywhere and find a morsel to chew on. This book is different. It begins with the basic tools that every manager must master and leads you steadily to increasingly more complicated situations and advanced techniques. It's meant to be read from start to finish.

With that caveat in mind, let's get started.

CHAPTER 1

How Anyone Can Manage Me

Reduced to its essence, there really is only one management principle that works: Do unto others as you would have them do unto you. This is the Golden Rule. It's been drilled into all of us since childhood. Unfortunately, few of us practice it as well as we preach it.

A big reason, I suspect, is that few of us have ever stepped back and enumerated exactly how we would want to be managed ourselves. And even if we did construct this list of ideal management behavior, I suspect there is a considerable gap between what we want from our boss and how we operate as a boss ourselves.

I've never fooled myself into thinking that I could practice the Golden Rule 100 percent of the time. None of us is a saint. None of us is perfect. But if you're looking for a foolproof indicator of how you're doing as a manager, calculating the gap between how you want to be managed and *how you actually manage* is a good place to start. But before you do unto others, you must know how you would have them do unto you.

Here's how anyone can manage me.

1. BE CONSISTENT.

Bosses want their subordinates to be consistent and reliable. When they give an order, they need to know that it will be carried out, not forgotten or delayed. This expectation, which is the foundation of the chain of command, also works the other way. Subordinates want their bosses to be consistent and reliable.

For example, people who know me well know I'm obsessed with time. Where other people function in increments of days or hours ("I'll call you on Thursday"), my increments are minutes and seconds ("Meet me at 11:20").

I've always thought this was a mixed blessing for me as a manager. On the one hand, it makes me efficient and forces others to match my efficiency. But it's also frustrating, particularly when I have to deal with people who are considerably more cavalier with time than I am. I sometimes judge people harshly and unfairly because their inner clocks are at odds with mine.

But there's a hidden virtue in my time obsession. Earlier this year I was scheduled to phone one of our executives at home at 7:30 on Sunday morning and was running ten minutes late. Now, I have a hunch most people in that situation would simply call when they could. There's enough give in most of our schedules to accommodate ten minutes of tardiness. But I didn't know what this fellow had planned for the rest of his morning. So at precisely 7:30 I called to tell him I would be ten minutes late. A part of me felt sheepish doing this, as if I had taken my time obsession to a comical extreme. But this executive thanked me and pointed out that my obsession with time management was more a luxury than a nuisance for him—because he knew that I would do what I said I would do. If nothing else, I was consistent.

That's infinitely better than working for someone who says he'll talk to you at ten o'clock and then you don't hear from him all day. He calls two days later and, barely apologizing, says, "Oh yeah, I forgot about the call. It wasn't that important."

I know I would appreciate it. A boss who keeps his promises and consistently does what he says he'll do can manage me.

2. GIVE ME CLEAR RATHER THAN VAGUE OBJECTIVES.

And translate those objectives into benefits for me.

A lot of managers try to make a virtue out of being vague or ambiguous. They circle the subject so their subordinates will learn to think for themselves. That works in problem-solving situations, where you're trying to create independent thinkers. But it's pure chaos when you are laying out goals for your people to accomplish. Subordinates don't respond to ambiguity about what they are expected to do.

A boss who not only told me exactly what I needed to do but who gave me the feeling that if I did it I would benefit in some way (a raise, a promotion, an extra week of vacation) could easily manage me.

3. GIVE ME A REASONABLE MIDDLE-TERM CAREER PATH.

I would never expect a boss to tell me where my career would be in ten years if I did everything I was asked to do. Too much can happen in ten years. But I would expect a manager with authority to know what's in store for me two years down the road. A boss who cannot tell me where I'll be in two years is basically saying I'm on my own. That's not the way to manage me.

4. GIVE ME LOTS OF ROPE (BUT DON'T LET GO).

Managers run between two extremes. On one side are the control freaks who have to dominate every aspect of their employees' activities. They care about the hours you keep, the people you talk to, the way you write your letters, even the way you dress. This martinet style works sometimes. On the other side are the laissez-faire types who are totally results-oriented and don't question anything as long as the results are delivered. They give you wide latitude to make things happen.

I prefer a boss who gives me wide latitude, but does so out of calculation rather than lack of interest or lack of thought. I would respond well to a boss who says, "I don't care what time you show up in the morning as long as you are producing. Just let me know the people you are calling on before the fact, not after. I might be able to help." I would worry about a boss who said the same thing but left out the offer to help.

5. DON'T MAKE ME GUESS WHEN YOU'RE UNHAPPY.

I would want to know immediately that my boss was un-happy—and why. And I'd want him to tell me outright, not make me guess.

Unfortunately, some bosses have problems expressing their displeasure. They sit on their unhappiness, hoping it will go away. Or they alter their behavior slightly, assuming their employees can read their minds. More often than not, these methods don't work. Until it is out in the open, the un-happiness only festers and grows.

If I'm doing something wrong, I want my boss to tell me as soon as possible. Nothing would irritate me more than a boss letting me do something in a particular manner for a long time uncorrected, letting me think that it was acceptable, and then, after the tenth time I've committed the same er-ror, exploding at me for my stupidity.

The stupidity isn't mine alone. And it's not the way to manage me.

6. MAKE ME FEEL LIKE AN OWNER.

Not everyone can be an owner. Some enterprises are not de-signed to be shared. But I would always want the feeling that I was an "owner" (even when I'm not).

A lot of managers have an easy solution for this. When things are going well, they pay their people well. They share the spoils of victory when they can afford it.

The true test of a boss who makes me feel like an owner, though, is when things are not going well. Does the boss make the same sacrifices—the pay cut, the reduced budget, the longer hours—that I'm being asked to make? If the boss announces that we have to cut expenses and overhead by 10 percent, does he feel exempt from that edict when it suits his fancy? Or does he stick to it, even though he has the authority and equity to do whatever he pleases?

A boss who shares the suffering as well as the spoils can always manage me.

● ● ●

THE MCCORMACK RULES

- Reduced to its essence, there really is only one management principle that works: Do unto others as you would have them do unto you. This is the Golden Rule.

- Before you do unto others you must know how you would have them do unto you.

- A boss who keeps his promises and consistently does what he says he'll do can manage anyone.

- Most people prefer a boss who gives them wide latitude, but only if the boss does so out of calculation rather than lack of interest or lack of thought.

CHAPTER 2

The Tools at Your Disposal

LEADERSHIP BEGINS WITH A FEW CORE BELIEFS

It used to be that a manager had only three things to worry about at work: the *people* reporting to him; the *work* they did; and the *money* coming in and going out. You could add a fourth item to this list—the *growth* of the business—but as long as the money coming in exceeded the money going out, growth usually took care of itself.

It's not that simple anymore. Managers have long passed the point where they can be masters of all the disciplines and subdisciplines of good management.

It's not enough to be a good judge and handler of people anymore. Today's managers need the theoretical underpinning of an industrial psychologist, the temperament of a human resources professional, and the litigation skills of an attorney.

The same is true with money, where it helps to be comfortable with the fine points of banking, finance, accounting, and taxation.

As for the work itself, it seems that every job requires that the boss become familiar with a personal computer.

With so much complexity and specialization in the workplace, it is impossible for a manager to be all things to all people. But every manager needs to function from a set of core beliefs. That's why it's essential for all managers to look inside themselves and figure out what makes them tick. In doing so, they will learn which managerial approaches to embrace and which to ignore. If you can't be all things to all people, at least you can be the right things to yourself. As a manager, the following are my core beliefs:

1. WORK HARDER THAN EVERYONE ELSE.

This is the reason I don't feel *too* guilty calling one of our executives at home at 5:30 A.M. or asking people to meet at the office on a weekend. I know our people know that I'm making the same sacrifices. I'm up as early as they are (in many cases, I'm calling from a different time zone where I'm awake even earlier) and I'm in the weekend meeting, too.

Working harder (or at least as hard) as everyone else gives a manager credibility. Without credibility, you cannot lead people. With credibility, everyone (and everything) follows.

2. Show people, then let them run with it.

There's a part of me that has always liked to lecture. After law school, I spent part of my military service as a law instructor. My business books grew out of instructional talks I regularly gave to our company. Not every manager has this didactic streak. But I do, and I'd be a fool to disown it.

Thus, when I think I know how to do something better than other people, I tell them about it. But there's a second part to this equation that's equally important: I don't instruct over and over again. I show people once (maybe twice if it's a subtle concept) and then assume they can handle it on their own.

Instruction is a core principle for me because, in a personal services business, duplicating a certain level of service is the biggest challenge. Showing people increases the chances that our people will do things the way I do them.

But getting out of the way is important, too. It helps a manager identify talent. The ones who learn have ability. The ones who don't have a learning disability.

3. Stay away unless you add value.

This is a corollary to "show them, then let them run with it." If managers can't be all things to all people, they also can't be everywhere at once. To maintain their sanity, they need to know when to jump into a situation and when to stay out.

My personal criterion is, "Do I add value to the situation?" It doesn't work 100 percent of the time. Sometimes I miscalculate the value of my involvement. But I have to believe our employees are stronger more as a result of the times I've stayed out of a situation than the times I've jumped in.

4. BE RUTHLESS ABOUT ONE THING, NOT EVERYTHING.

If you can't be all things to all people, you have to pick your spots. Once you get to a certain size in business, it's impossible to be relentless or obsessed with every detail of every situation under your command. I reached that point about twelve years ago when I realized that I no longer knew the name or face of everyone who worked in our company and that I could no longer have my finger on the pulse of every deal in every division. The company was simply too big.

So I stopped needing to know about everything and narrowed it down to one thing.

In my case, I've become ruthless about costs. I am willing to throw myself into the minutiae of how we spend money internally—from travel expenses to purchase orders to vendors' contracts—with an intensity that I devote to few other managerial duties. When our cost structures get to where I want them to be, perhaps I'll become ruthless about something else. As a manager, it's my core belief that delving deeply into one problem area is better than skimming halfheartedly over a half dozen areas. In the former case, you can solve something. In the latter, I doubt if you solve anything at all.

5. LIGHTEN UP WHEN THINGS GET HEAVY.

Let's face it, a manager needs a sense of humor, if only because (a) its absence makes work dreary and (b) a lot of funny things happen on the job.

A sense of humor is never more valuable than in those dark moments in business when everyone is under intense pressure. A timely joke, a trenchant comment, or simply laughing about how bleak things have gotten won't cure the crisis. But your employees will feel better if they can see that you don't feel so bad.

HOW BUREAUCRACIES ARE BORN

If you want to see a Jekyll/Hyde side to my personality, just get me talking about bureaucracies. I probably go back and forth on the subject more than anything else I do as a manager.

On the one hand, I hate bureaucracies. As I look around our company, I realize it is now impossible for me to personally know all of our 2000 employees. That bothers me. I get a sentimental longing for the early days of our company when it was just four or five people and myself in a couple of rooms in Cleveland. There were no policies, no committees, no job titles, no income projections, and very few memos. I was a complete hands-on manager—because everyone and everything was literally at my fingertips. Plus, I felt I had my finger on the pulse of everything we were doing. If a client won a tournament over the weekend, the energy and tempo of the office would visibly increase on Monday—and I could see it.

On the other hand, I need bureaucracies. The simple fact that I don't know everyone in the company virtually demands that we install the rules, committees, procedures, and personnel that make up a bureaucracy. Bureaucracies give me a sense of control over an organization that's really beyond my control.

I suspect I share my ambivalence about bureaucracies with any manager of a growing company. We all want to maintain the turn-on-a-dime agility of a start-up company even as we're pushing the organization harder and harder to maintain rapid growth. But in order to control the bureaucracy that's slowly but steadily growing under our feet, we first have to understand how bureaucracies are born.

1. QUESTION TRADITION.

Traditions are a great breeding ground for bureaucracies.

When we were a small company, several of us in senior positions read all the documents, memos, and telexes that came in each day. It was a good and manageable method to keep us fully informed. Over time, as the company grew and the number of documents grew, this tradition spawned an elaborate internal mechanism of paper-gathering and photocopying to make sure these same people continued to see all the documents, even though they no longer had a need to see them and, in fact, were throwing them away unread.

I was guilty of this myself. It took me a longer than I'd like to admit to realize I didn't need to see all the faxes. But that's the trouble with traditions. You get into a habit of doing something and, though the original reason for doing it has long disappeared, you continue to do it because you have always done it.

No one steps back in time to question a tradition, and before you know it, you've built an elaborate machine to perform a task that doesn't need performing.

2. BEWARE THE INTERNAL POLICY THAT GREW.

The most fertile breeding grounds for bureaucracies are internal policies.

There's a dangerous mentality of dealing with problems by trying to lay out a rule that can fix all situations. That is a very bureaucratic thing to do. Rather than trying to be flexible in getting a sensible solution to a particular problem, bureaucracies tend to install broadbrush solutions that don't always comport with reality. Inevitably, the policy ends up being misconstrued or abused.

For example, we have a rule that the company pays the taxi fare home for non-executive staffers (*i.e.*, secretaries, clericals, etc.) who stay at work past 8 P.M. After a while, though, it turned out that people who finished their work at 7:15 or 7:30 P.M. would stay at their desk until eight o'clock doing nothing simply to get the taxi fare. A policy designed as a courtesy for people working long hours ended up being a discourtesy to the company.

Every year I try to find one or two rules that made sense when we started them but over time ended up achieving the opposite of what we intended. When I find them, I change them. It's the only way to keep the bureaucracy from getting out of control.

If you want to know how your bureaucracy is doing, take a random look at one of your seemingly minor operating policies. You might be surprised to learn how people are interpreting it.

3. Practice eternal vigilance.

Eternal vigilance is the only answer to controlling a bureaucracy.

One reason I liked to see all the documents running through our company is that I've found internal memos to be very revealing about our bureaucracy.

I try to read between the lines of intra-corporate memos with one eye on what they're saying and one eye out for signs of conflict in our company, particularly tension between corporate staff and our line executives.

Not long ago I saw a memo where one of our staff accounting people was chastising a young line executive for not following certain reporting procedures in closing a sale.

That sort of conflict between line and staff worries me—because it means the bureaucracy has lost its way. On the surface, the line executive was wrong; he forgot to cross some t's and dot some i's. The only problem was that he ran into the staff person in charge of crossing t's and dotting i's.

It's not surprising this happens. As your business becomes more complicated, you can't avoid adding support personnel such as accountants, data processing experts, and facility managers. You need these people to supply information and maintain controls. They are the heart and soul of a bureaucracy.

But, like any bureaucracy, these corporate staffs have a remarkable capacity to self-perpetuate and swell. If you're not careful, they can usurp the powers of your line executives. Pretty soon your corporate staff is establishing procedures, setting policy, and creating forms—mostly to talk to each other—and requiring line executives to comply with their forms.

That's when I have to remind employees that in the tug-of-war between line executives and staff, I will always be pulling for the people on the line. In our business, they are the ones knocking on doors, bringing in business, and maintaining relationships. They're in the best position to make decisions. And they, not the bureaucracy, will get my support.

COUNT YOUR CORE BUSINESSES WITH CARE

One of the toughest problems of being an entrepreneur is knowing what your core business is—and being sufficiently disciplined so you never lose sight of that core business as you try to grow your company and head off into more profitable areas. More entrepreneurs than I can count have been undone by their reckless expansion into ventures that on the surface seemed to be a part of their core business but, in fact, were nothing of the kind.

Most of the time, the easiest way to keep your eye on the core business is to keep telling yourself and your people what that core is.

For example, our company has been expanding so rapidly in the last five years that every eighteen months we find it necessary to hold indoctrination meetings to explain the various parts of the company to our new executives.

The last time we did this we flew over 200 people to Cleveland for three days, where they heard our senior executives explain what their respective divisions do. It was an impressive series of presentations, with a lot of big-dollar numbers being tossed around.

But at the end, I felt compelled to make a brief summary speech. I told the group that, despite all the big numbers they had heard, I didn't want them to forget that the core of our business has always been and always will be servicing the athlete clients. Without the athletes, you cannot create events. Without the events, you don't have sponsors. Without the sponsors, you don't have revenues. Without the revenues, you don't have profits and growth. Everything begins and ends with the athletes.

I wasn't throwing cold water on the festivities. I just wanted everyone there to keep their eye on the core.

Having said that, however, I think you have to be a little daring and imaginative in how you define your core business.

I once knew an entrepreneur who had a successful printing business specializing in crossword puzzle publications. At some point this entrepreneur started buying up crossword puzzle magazines.

I thought he was crazy to expand this way. Printing magazines is one thing. Publishing them, with all the editorial and marketing challenges they present, is another. He was veering away from his core business.

What I failed to appreciate was how he defined his core business. He had analyzed his company and concluded that he had a major problem: His two plants were profitable but they were only running at 50 percent capacity. In the printing industry, this can be ruinous. You want your presses running all the time. The ideal is a plant that's open twenty-four hours a day with three shifts.

His solution: Since he couldn't find more magazines as customers, he started buying magazines that were using other printers and converting them into customers. He had defined his core business not simply as printing, but printing 24 hours a day. The magazines were a clever (albeit risky) way to keep feeding his core business. As it turned out, the risk was minimal. The magazines were well-managed and ran themselves, and with the reduced expense of in-house printing, they were more efficient and profitable than ever.

I'm sure there are people in our company who questioned my sanity when we decided to venture into the representation of classical musicians ten or twelve years ago. What did this have to do with our core of athletes? But once you start thinking of concert violinists and lyric sopranos as performers—just as golfers and tennis players are performers—the similarities are irresistible.

- Musicians, like athletes, perform their art around the world without language considerations.

- Musicians face the same tax problems around the world that athletes do, and we were already equipped to handle that.

- Companies that were spending money in sports were also spending it on cultural events. We had good contacts among these companies. They trusted us when we said we could create and deliver a good event, whether it was a concert or a tennis tournament.

- We knew how to deal with temperamental clients and their boyfriends, girlfriends, husbands, wives, mothers, fathers, and hangers-on, and that too was prevalent in the classical music business.

- As with baseball, basketball, and football players, the compensation for classical artists was skyrocketing.

- Finally, we were multinational, whereas no one else in classical music had a legitimate network of overseas offices.

All these factors together took us to the point where we felt comfortable that classical music could become a core business for us. Today, with more than 100 employees in our IMG Artists division, it seems our instinct was correct.

That's one of the beautiful things about keeping your eye on your core business. You begin to understand it better than anyone else—and that's what gives you the insight and freedom to keep on growing.

THE TROUBLE WITH
ORGANIZATION CHARTS

After the introductory meeting, customers who want to know more about our company invariably ask to see two types of documents: our client roster and our organization chart.

I can understand why they ask for these documents. The client roster establishes our credibility. It tells prospects what kind of company they will be traveling in and reassures them that we are as good as we claim to be. The organization chart is valuable, too. In the sense that it reveals who reports to whom, who has power and who doesn't, it gives outsiders a road map of how to do business with us.

In both cases we say no, because we don't *have* a client roster or an organization chart.

There's a simple reason we don't publish a client roster. I don't want our competitors to use it against us. Most companies that publish their client list use it as a bragging license. The quality and depth of their roster lets them tell the world, "Hey, we're pretty good. Look at all these blue chip clients who work with us." To me, publishing a client list is like giving your competition a fishing license *and* pointing out all the good fishing holes. If it's a big list, smaller competitors can use our size against us in recruiting new clients ("They're so big, you'll get lost there"). If it's a complete list, the whole world may get ideas about poaching on our turf.

The reasons we don't draw up an organization chart are more complicated, but they all stem from a belief that such diagrams tend to defeat rather than promote good management. Here are four troubling features of organizational charts.

1. THEY PROMOTE FATTER, NOT FLATTER, STRUCTURES.

The moment you try to codify the various layers of management in your organization, you can be sure that your people will try to improve it. And "improvement" rarely means shrinking the structure. If you construct a hierarchy where executives measure themselves by how few people are above them and how many people are below them, you shouldn't be surprised that the structure tends to grow vertically. People add layers in order to elevate themselves.

My friend Ben Bidwell, who developed his expertise on corporate structures as the chairman of Chrysler Motors, likes to quote the Japanese on the subject: "The flatter the structure, the better it will stand in the wind." I like that. As Bidwell constantly reminds me, "Five levels of management are infinitely better than fifteen" (if only because you save on water jugs and private bathrooms). There's no optimum number. Companies differ in terms of products, integration levels, distribution systems, and sheer size. But there is an optimum target: as few levels as possible.

In that sense, the only reason to draw an organizational chart is to help you decide which layers to eliminate.

2. They don't inspire teamwork.

In theory, committing the chain of command to paper should promote teamwork and cooperation. But quite often, it does the opposite. When people can literally see their position in the corporate hierarchy, they tend to protect that position rather than move freely up and down from level to level.

You see this all the time with executives who dramatically alter the way they communicate with a co-worker depending on that individual's rank. They're fawning and obsequious with their superiors, competitive and minimally cooperative with their peers, and barely tolerant with their inferiors.

I'd much rather have an amorphous corporate structure, where status and rank are intentionally vague. Instead of a clearly defined vertical or pyramidal chain of command, the structure would resemble a circle. It would be like having a meeting at a round table. Everyone is equal. Everyone can see each other. Anyone can speak up at any time.

That structure would inspire cooperation.

3. THEY DON'T CREATE STABILITY.

This is perhaps the greatest argument against organizational charts. People draft them to illustrate an organization's stability. But I don't see how they motivate people positively or contribute to the organization's stability.

I don't mean to give the impression that our company of 2000 people is completely disorganized. It isn't. The heads of our various line and staff divisions are clearly defined. But we don't go overboard on spelling out who is filling each division's #2, #3, #4 slots and so on down the line. In my experience, naming names on a depth chart creates more friction and backbiting than cooperation. Suddenly you have scenarios where #4 wants #3's job, #3 is doing everything to stifle #4, and they're all gunning for #2. I'd much rather have five people think they're all tied for the #2 slot. People work harder for the company's benefit when they only have to worry about what the person in the #1 slot thinks.

4. THEY DESTROY THE MYSTERY.

If I were trying to sell a big idea to a big company, my greatest asset would be an insider's guide to that company's chain of command. This chart would tell me who reports to whom and who can make decisions and who can't. Reading between the lines, I could probably pick up a few clues about the company's key players and their interlocking relationships with one another. With that road map in hand, I'd have a tremendous negotiating advantage.

Conversely, people doing business with us would have a similar advantage with a road map of our company. This may be the strongest argument for keeping an air of mystery around your organizational chart. The mystery gives you an edge.

P.S.: Although we don't publish a client list or organizational chart, we do hand out a yearly calendar of events that we own, organize, manage, produce for television, or represent. It's a mighty revealing document. For example, on the third Sunday in March of this year, a reader would learn that we are involved with the Nestlé Invitational golf tournament in Orlando, Florida; three separate ski events in Spain, the Czech Republic, and Vail, Colorado; an international cricket test match in Guyana; the Portuguese stop on the European PGA tour; a "Discover Card Stars on Ice" show in Syracuse, New York; a field hockey championship in Lahore, Pakistan; the Lipton Tennis Championships in Key Biscayne, Florida; a production of *West Side Story* in Melbourne, Australia; the World Figure Skating Championships in Chiba, Japan; the short track speed skating team championships in Cambridge, Canada; and a production of *Jesus Christ Superstar* in Wellington, New Zealand.

If people are curious about your company, rather than telling them who you work for or how you're organized, I think it's much better to tell them what you actually do.

FOUR FORMS OF PERSUASION

As the founder and CEO of a company, I have always thought that I could get anything to happen at our company if I wanted it to happen. No matter how foolish or whimsical my personal decision may be, I could push it through the organization simply by dictating that it be done. In theory, like any boss, all I would have to say is, "Do it!"

But I don't.

For one thing, barking commands is not my idea of fun. It not only wears down the people being barked at, it wears down the person doing the barking. It is also a tough act to keep going over the long term. After so many edicts and tirades, people eventually tune you out.

Demanding and dictating also tends to defeat one of the main goals of a manager—namely, getting people to support an idea that they will have to execute without you. I learned long ago that if you tell people to do something that they really don't want to do, no matter how great your authority or how severely you may punish them for disobeying you, there is always a degree of resentment, a feeling of "We'll show the boss how wrong he is." That resentment may vary in degree—from benign neglect of the command to willfully sabotaging it—but it is there just the same.

The most compelling reason that I don't say "Do it!" that often, though, is the simple fact that I have other subtle forms of persuasion that are more effective and certainly less wearisome. On the following page begins a list of my four favorites.

1. CASUAL PERSUASION.

If you have a good idea, you can usually improve its chances of coming to life if you can convince someone else that it's their idea as well. Casual persuasion is the act of dropping an idea in someone's lap and then helping them to notice it.

Quite often, if I have an idea that I want one of our executives to implement, I will casually mention it in a conversation. I don't flag it by saying, "Here's a great idea!" I simply muse out loud in the hope that an alert listener might pick up on it. Then I wait for something good to happen.

If the employee doesn't get back to me on it in a week or two, I'll casually bring it up again the next time we talk. Chances are, he'll have forgotten all about it. He might say, "Gee, I didn't realize you were serious about this." Then we'll move on to another subject. A few days later I might send him a memo with some additional thoughts or a news clipping that relates to the idea. After a few weeks of this soft but relentless prodding, even the most unresponsive employee will get the hint that I want something to happen. But I haven't pounded the idea into him. I've given him several weeks to let the idea slowly soak in. When the employee actually brings the concept to life, he invariably thinks it's his idea. I see no reason to disagree.

2. TEXTBOOK PERSUASION.

Textbook persuasion means teaching or showing people how to do things your way.

I wasn't aware I did this until someone pointed it out to me. I was having an informal lunch with a small group of employees at a golf tournament. One of them mentioned a contract he was negotiating in the Far East. Apparently, the lawyer in me came to the fore and I started peppering him with questions about the contract—queries about automatic renewal options, insurance clauses, escalating royalties, and several other nuggets that I consider essential to a good contract. That was my not-so-subtle way of persuading him to do it my way. If he hadn't considered all those nuggets before that lunch, I'm sure he corrected it shortly thereafter.

In hindsight, this instructive urge has probably been my favorite form of persuasion. In the 1970s and 1980s, when I wasn't sure that all the new executives in our growing company were negotiating contracts or servicing clients or selling certain properties in the IMG way, I started giving regular lectures on those specific subjects.

Quite often I would take it a step further. If I wanted to persuade someone to accept my ideas on client service, I would actually take them into a meeting and show them how to deal with a client.

3. THIRD-PARTY PERSUASION.

I've always tried to hire people smarter than I am in specific areas. In our company, dozens of people are smarter in their area of expertise than I'll ever be. That's a foolproof hiring policy, but it also presents a management problem—particularly when you're trying to persuade the expert to accept *your* idea in his or her area of expertise. That's when it's prudent to use a third party.

If I have the greatest idea in the world for a television program, I might suggest it to the head of our television division. Of course, I am not a programming wizard—I know about as much as the average citizen—and that colors how my suggestion is perceived. My idea would probably get a far better reception if it came from a third party, from someone our television head respected as an expert in broadcasting.

If you don't have the credibility to keep a good idea moving, find a third party.

4. DEADLINE PERSUASION.

Giving people deadlines to do something is one step shy of saying, "Do it!" It's not very subtle, but it's persuasive.

There will always be situations where you don't have the luxury or time to (a) let an idea seep slowly into a person's intellect, or (b) instruct an employee, or (c) find a third party to deliver your message. That's when I resort to deadlines. Not long ago I learned that we had a unique opportunity to acquire a sports event for a very good price. To persuade our people who would actually run the event that this was a good idea would have taken weeks or months. But we didn't have the time to wait. In a few weeks the event's price would have tripled, and someone else might have acquired it.

So I gave our people a deadline: "If we don't go in tomorrow and buy it, someone else will."

If you can't persuade people on the merits of a concept, you can usually do it by stressing its urgency.

A Company's Second Tier Reveals Its True Strength

People tell me that one of our company's strengths is the layer of senior executives right below me. Every one of these executives can play in the major leagues.

I wish I could take credit for knowing that things would turn out so well. But I can't. When I hired each of them twenty years ago, I wasn't thinking about creating an effective second tier in our organization. I needed each of them for their specific skills in a particular area such as television, tennis, golf, or finance. The business grew, they grew, and the two meshed. Those are the mechanics of it.

In hindsight, however, I think there are certain guidelines for any manager who wants a company that's built to last.

1. Pile on the work.

I don't like to "Peter Principle" people. That is, I won't promote a great salesperson to sales manager simply to reward him for selling well. I'd rather keep that person selling *and* give him other things to do. The best people tend to respond to this sort of challenge. It taps unknown resources. When the workload gets too heavy, they're smart enough to find help (usually by hiring people and enlarging their own empire).

2. BREAK THE MOLD.

I also like to give executives responsibilities that, on the surface at least, run counter to their expertise or expectations.

One of our senior people has been an avid skier all his life. When he joined our company twenty four years ago, he expected to work in our fledgling winter sports division. Instead, I assigned him to golf—so he could first learn how our company did things in an area where we were well-established. Then he could apply those principles in skiing. In effect, he learned to do business in two sports in the time it took to master one.

3. GIVE THEM AUTONOMY.

You can't develop leaders unless you let them lead. This means not only letting them make their own calls, but stepping aside even when you suspect they're wrong.

4. GIVE THEM ROOM TO ERR—BUT NOT TWICE.

This is the corollary to giving people autonomy. You can't blame people for taking risks and failing. That's part of the learning process. But if they make the same mistake twice, you have yourself to blame.

5. LET THEM THINK IT'S THEIR IDEA.

If there is any doubt about who deserves the credit for a corporate success, let your people take it. Your ego can stand it.

Your associates will appreciate it. And the company will profit from it.

6. STEP DOWN SO THEY CAN STEP UP.

Part of being the boss in our company means that I am in a constant process of shedding certain responsibilities. It means clearly establishing that what was once my job is now theirs.

For example, the golf division is one of the mainstays of our company, and for years I headed up our activities in golf. But I no longer do that. I don't manage golfers. I don't travel on the tour. I don't have line responsibilities. I don't run golf division meetings. Someone else has that job now. I've stepped aside because that's the only way our senior people can step up and grow.

7. PAY THEM WELL.

Being generous with praise, advancement, recognition, and responsibility may help build a winning team, but unless you pay them what they're worth, there's no guarantee that you can keep them. Your senior people, by definition, should be making substantial contributions to the company. They're entitled to more than the satisfaction of a job well done.

SPEED SOLVES A LOT OF PROBLEMS

Not long ago I sent some of my syndicated columns to Jack Welch, the chairman and CEO of General Electric, including a story that had the fanciful concept of dividing employees into thoroughbreds and plowhorses. My point in the story (and the reason for the equine analogy) was that thoroughbred employees are blessed with speed. If you give them an order, they do it right away. They can do in one day what a plowhorse would need a week to finish. The next time Welch wrote to me, he circled that paragraph on speed and wrote in the margin, "This is what I have to work on." Of all the qualities the chairman of GE could focus on, speed was first in his mind.

I think if you ask most CEOs, they'd agree. Everything else being equal, speed slaughters the competition.

It's certainly true in sports. In football, tennis, or baseball, superior foot speed can help you outrun a defender, chase down a sure winner, or beat out a throw that would catch a slower runner. There's a big difference between speed in sports and in business. In sports you can't teach speed; you're either born fast or you aren't. In business you can teach people to speed up.

It isn't simple, though. You can't develop corporate speed by ordering your people to "Do it faster!" You inevitably pay with that approach, usually with burned-out employees or diminished quality. Here are five tactics that can make you more nimble without tripping you up.

1. ELIMINATE THE APPROVAL PROCESS.

The chain of command can be the biggest boost or the biggest obstacle to corporate speed.

If you're racing your competition to develop a hot new product and your engineers have to go through five layers of management to get a design change or revised budget approved, your chain of command is not speeding things up. It's slowing you down. I suspect that if you analyzed the time it takes to get a new product out the door, at least half of that time is wasted in corporate limbo while your most talented people wait for someone's signature or approval.

I'm not suggesting that you give your people carte blanche, that there's no value in corporate oversight. But if good ideas come to life slowly in your company and your rivals consistently beat you to the finish line, chances are your bureaucracy is the culprit. You can gain anywhere from hours to months on your competition with one swift stroke if you eliminate it.

2. SET SLIGHTLY UNREALISTIC DEADLINES.

Too many managers let fat creep into their timetables. If they think they can complete a project in three weeks under optimal conditions (*i.e.*, if everything goes like clockwork), they'll give themselves and their employees four weeks—because they know things go wrong. (A customer can change the order. A supplier can be a day late with a delivery.) They think they're being responsible and realistic by factoring in all the things that can slow the project down. But being realistic is no way to add speed to an organization.

I'd rather give them a slightly unrealistic schedule—say, twelve working days to finish the project instead of fifteen. If you push people, within reason and in small increments, to work faster, don't be surprised if they meet your target. Likewise, if you pad your deadlines, don't be surprised when your people slow down to meet your expectations.

37

3. STICK TO THE TIMETABLE.

A deadline is meaningless if you don't constantly hang it over people's heads and enforce it. There's no point in setting a slightly unrealistic deadline if your people don't believe that there is no excuse, short of an act of God, for missing it.

4. PRACTICE WHAT YOU PREACH.

People take their timing and pacing cues from the top. If you want your people to operate at an accelerated rate, you have to function at least at their speed—and probably faster.

I'm sure speed is a priority at our company because it is a priority to me. I pride myself on little displays of speediness—on returning phone calls as soon as possible or on fulfilling a promise within a day or two where others might take a week or more. I'm constantly looking for more efficient ways to use my time—whether it's urging a long-winded talker to get to the point in a meeting or debating with a driver about the fastest route to my next meeting. And that filters down to the employees who deal with me on a regular basis. It's understandable that they will try hard to keep up with me.

You can't expect to have a fast, nimble organization if you aren't fast and nimble yourself—and constantly striving to get faster.

5. TEAMWORK INCREASES SPEED.

It may sound obvious, but a team of ten people can get something done a lot faster than one person working alone. Of course, if it's so obvious, why are there so many solo acts in most organizations and so few teams?

One reason, I suspect, is that managers don't always appreciate the urgency of some situations and the need to disrupt everything in the organization in order to deal with that situation as quickly as possible. Another reason: They don't appreciate the accelerating effect of a team. A person working alone will work at his own pace. A person working within a team will try to keep up with the team's fastest member.

I came to appreciate this more than twenty-five years ago when our golf client, Tony Jacklin, won the 1970 U.S. Open the year after he became a national hero in Great Britain for winning the British Open. I realized that if we were ever going to maximize Jacklin's commercial appeal in the U.S. the way we did in the U.K., there would never be a better time than when he was the reigning U.S. Open champion. I also realized that no one individual could call on all the companies in all the categories in that narrow time frame.

So I gathered all our executives in Cleveland and told them to drop everything for Jacklin. They had two weeks to drum up deals for Jacklin. Then I went around the room and gave each executive a specific category that had endorsement potential—everything from golf equipment to automakers to luggage manufacturers to soft-drink companies. I was stunned with all the offers they came back with two weeks later. Part of it, I'm sure, was the air of urgency imparted by the slightly unrealistic two-week deadline. But a bigger reason was the competitive effect on the team. No one on the team wanted to be the only one who came back empty-handed.

THREE THINGS TO DO SLOWLY

As a result of all this emphasis on speed, we now live in an accelerated age, where the tendency is to do things more quickly rather than slowly.

A big reason, of course, is all the new technology at our disposal. Express mail, faxes, supersonic jets, modems, and cellular phones, in theory, have added hours of productivity to our business day and speeded up our response time. There's nothing wrong with that. I like being able to conduct a full morning of business in London, board a late morning Concorde from Heathrow, and be in my New York office by 11 A.M.

But the fact that people and technology are urging us to do things faster doesn't necessarily mean it's good. There's something to be said for stepping back occasionally, catching our breath, and reexamining some of our activities which might be better done slowly.

For example, hiring decisions obviously should be made slowly—because you're literally inviting a stranger into your company, and that demands some reflection. But more often than not, people tend to hire in haste, because they desperately need someone to fill the open position. They don't ask, Does this job need a replacement? They don't reinvent the job description. They just look for someone who resembles the departing employee.

Acquiring new technology is certainly another area where you're better off waiting rather than rushing in. A cellular phone that cost $2000 five years ago can be yours for $200 now—and it will be a better phone. When it comes to gadgets and computers, nothing is more expensive now than it was one or two years ago. Most people know this. But nowhere near as many people can resist the urge to buy it today and wait for prices to come down tomorrow.

The fact is, we all know we should do some things more slowly. But we don't. Here, for starters, are three things I always remind myself to do more slowly. Once you recognize how the rest of the world is trying to speed you up against your best interests, you'll begin to see the merits of slow motion in a lot of hasty behavior.

1. INTRUDE ON A RELATIONSHIP SLOWLY.

Any change in a personal business relationship should be done with measured care rather than haste.

A good example in our company would be injecting a third party into an ongoing successful personal relationship between a client and his manager. Let's say that you are the account supervisor of a superstar athlete who is counting on you personally to handle all his affairs. Let's also say that the skills you display in handling this superstar have convinced top management to increase your executive responsibilities. As a result, you have less time to devote to your superstar. Obviously, you need a replacement to handle the superstar. In my experience, people can be clumsy in how they inject this replacement into the superstar relationship. Yes, they think about who they're going to assign to the job, but, in their hurry to move on to bigger things, they tend to rush the process. They don't take enough time to prepare the client for a change or shape events so the client thinks the change is his idea.

If a decision affects the feelings of another person, take your time announcing it. The more important that person is, the more time you'll need.

41

I remember some years ago when one of our New York executives needed to get out of an agent/manager relationship with a top golf client. He didn't know how to do it, until one day he noticed that three out of every four phone calls he received from this golfer involved financial questions—about taxes, insurance, asset sales in his various side businesses, etc.—which he wasn't qualified to answer. So he identified a young financial wizard in our Cleveland office. Whenever the client had a financial question, he would set up a three-way conference call that included the young executive. After a year of this, the golfer took the bait and started calling the financial wizard directly—but only on money matters. It took three years before the golfer was fully weaned away from the New York executive and happy to put his affairs in the hands of the young Cleveland executive. But, quite often, you need that much time to build a new relationship. Taking any less may very well destroy it.

Remember this the next time you think you can hand over a customer relationship to a colleague or subordinate. No matter how talented and charming your replacement may be, no matter how strenuously you assure the customer that you'll be around to keep an eye on things, you have to give the customer time to get used to the idea.

2. SIGN CONTRACTS SLOWLY.

There are a lot of compelling reasons to sign a contract sooner rather than later. If everyone agrees on the essential deal points, it's nice to have a fully executed agreement before someone changes their mind. But I always worry when the other side is rushing me to sign a contract. Their haste is a red flag that reminds me to take great care reviewing the agreement. The faster they want me to move, the slower I tend to go.

Of course, a skilled dealmaker on the other side doesn't explicitly hurry you to sign a contract. He doesn't say, "Sign this by next week." He has cannier, more insidious ways to rush you.

One of the more common ploys is waiting until the last few weeks of the year to send out a draft of the agreement. Some people feel compelled to sign such a contract before December 31—for perfectly legitimate reasons. They might want to receive the money within the fiscal year for tax purposes or so they can meet a sales quota. But that sort of contractual time-bomb is no reason to hastily agree to terms that don't suit you.

In fact, other parties have tried this end-of-the-year contract ploy on our clients so often that we have come up with an elegant but simple defense. We tell the other side that they haven't given us much time to review the agreement, that we'll need at least a few weeks into the new year to work it out. But we tell them that we fully intend to sign it once the details have been worked out, and then we ask them to advance us part of the guaranteed payment during the current fiscal year. We even offer them an "Intention to Sign" letter as a sign of good faith, stipulating that if we fail to agree by a set date, the money will be returned. It's a nice win-win. The other side risks nothing. Our client gets paid quickly. But most important, a less-than-perfect contract is not jammed down our throats.

3. CONFRONT SLOWLY.

We all know it's dumb to send off a letter written in anger and haste, that it's better to put it in a drawer for twenty-four hours to see if you feel the same way the next day. It's the same with confrontation.

Yet few people practice this. They think any challenge or personal attack in the workplace requires instant retaliation, as if letting the attack go unchecked for a day or a week somehow undermines their position. In a highly public forum this may be the right move. Politicians during an election campaign, for example, know that they must instantly respond to any attacks from their opponent. The longer they wait, the more likely the charges will stick. But electoral politics is not the same as office politics. In the workplace, confrontation should be taken slowly.

In our company I see enough decisions that I disagree with each day that I could literally spend my entire day correcting or confronting the people who made those decisions. But I don't. For one thing, I've learned that effective confrontation is a function of effective timing. I've waited weeks, months, sometimes years to confront some people about their questionable behavior. Rarely has the delay hurt me or the company. In so many cases, the problem corrected itself or simply became moot as business conditions changed. In every case, waiting has also taken some of the emotion and personal animus out of the confrontation. It frees me up to deal rationally with the problem rather than the person. That's a great luxury if you're managing a lot of talented, independent-minded people. You only earn that luxury if you learn how to wait.

PESSIMISM PAYS WHEN IT COMES TO TIME

Nothing fascinates me more than people's capacity to delude themselves. They think they're smarter, funnier, more athletic, more articulate, more charming than they really are. We're all guilty of this.

Fortunately, most of our self-delusions don't cause that much damage in business. Overestimating how articulate we really are might make us look like a preening boor to some people, but it doesn't derail a career. I know plenty of people who take great delight in hearing themselves talk. As far as I can tell, this personality flaw hasn't prevented them from being very successful.

But there's one area where our delusion (or inflated sense of optimism) can be dangerous. I'm talking about our sense of time. Nearly all of us have an inflated or overoptimistic sense of how much we can accomplish in a given amount of time. We schedule a meeting for one hour and it ends up taking two hours. We promise to get a proposal on the client's desk in two days and we still haven't finished it four days later. This delusion affects almost every activity in the business day: We think we can get to a meeting across town in twenty minutes, but heavy traffic or a wrong turn conspires against us; the trip takes thirty minutes.

None of us is immune to this delusion. If we managed our time as well as we think we do, all the items on our "to do" list would be completed at the end of every day. The awful truth is, we tend to be optimistic rather than pessimistic about how much we can accomplish in a day—and it costs us. Our inflated optimism irritates people, disappoints others, and in extreme cases ruins our credibility.

The quick cure, obviously, is to err on the side of pessimism in gauging our use of time. If you know you need twenty minutes to get across town under perfect conditions (i.e., no traffic, no red lights), assume it's an imperfect world and give yourself a ten minute cushion. Schedule thirty minutes for the trip. (It's a sign of how much we delude ourselves that many of us believe we can make the trip in fifteen minutes!)

In my heart, though, I don't believe people can go from being time optimists to pessimists overnight. It's like asking an alcoholic to quit drinking on the spot. A step-by-step program is usually more effective. With that in mind, here are six steps that can help each of us gauge our time more realistically.

1. ARE YOU WORKING WHEN YOU WORK?

This is my first question when people tell me they don't have enough time in the day to get their jobs done.

I know an editor/writer at a monthly magazine in New York whose sole responsibility is to edit a section of the magazine and write a thousand-word column each month. Yet whenever I call him at home on a weekend, I'm told he's holed up in his office working on his column. This has been going on for years. I asked him once if he enjoyed giving up his weekends to write the column. He said he hated it.

"So why don't you write it during the week?" I asked.

"Because I'm too busy having meetings, going out to lunch, talking on the phone, and pushing paper to get any work done," he said.

I suspect that's true for a lot of people in office jobs. Going to work offers so many distractions, they don't have time to do their real job.

The first step to getting a realistic grasp of your time is examining how you actually work when you're allegedly working.

2. ARE YOU DOING 100 PERCENT WHEN 90 PERCENT WILL DO?

Quite often, when people take two days to finish an assignment they expected to finish in one, it's because they spent the extra day trying to make it "perfect." They want to hand in something 100 percent acceptable when actually 90 percent will do.

I'm not advocating or excusing shoddy work. But it should make us reconsider which tasks require obsessive attention to detail and which don't. For example, I could spend fifty hours every week of my life on correspondence—from sales letters to internal memos to faxes to thank you notes to answering résumés. There's a part of me that wishes every document bearing my signature was as well written as I could make it.

But I decided a long time ago that I would rather get a hundred letters out that were 90 percent of my best than ninety letters that were 100 percent. I'd rather appear responsive to a hundred people than let ten items fall through the cracks. Massaging a memo until it gleams like a jewel just isn't worth the time or effort (and I suspect that no one is grading my writing style or holding the occasional typographical error against me).

I also suspect that we could all add hours of productive work to our week if we stepped back every so often and asked ourselves, "Do I really need to work this hard on this task? Will anyone notice my effort (or the lack of it)? Am I wasting time?"

3. ARE YOU A VICTIM OF TIME BANDITS?

Time bandits are all the people in your life who procrastinate, who are chronically late for appointments, who don't return phone calls, who take weeks to respond to a written query (if they respond at all). They steal your minutes, hours, and days by making you wait for them or by making you work three times harder just to talk to them. Time bandits are more deluded about the clock than anyone. And if you don't recognize the havoc they create, you're deluded, too.

Some people think they can make a time bandit change his ways. They're wrong. The person who shows up forty minutes late for your 10 A.M. appointment will always be late.

Some people refuse to deal with time bandits. That's not practical if the bandit is your client or boss or a valuable employee.

Most people are their victims—either because they don't recognize how the bandit is slowing them down or they think they can work around the bandit.

The best policy—at least the one that won't waste your time—is to refuse to be a victim.

I have a pretty good idea about the time sensitivity of most of the people I deal with on a regular basis. Maximizing my time is important to me, so I can't help noticing when other people share this trait (and when they don't). I factor this into everything I schedule with people. This isn't a particularly great achievement. Most of us do this all the time in social situations. If we're invited to a party, our knowledge of the host tells us whether we can be fashionably late or are expected to arrive promptly, and we act accordingly. Likewise, if we are hosting the party and expect guests to be prompt, we make a point of telling our chronically tardy friends, "Don't be late."

For some reason, people are not as alert or as willing to discipline time bandits in the workplace. If you're doing someone a favor by agreeing to meet with them for an hour between eleven o'clock and noon at your office and they are twenty minutes late, do you stick to your schedule or theirs? Do you politely end the meeting at noon and move on to the next item on your schedule or do you let it run over to accommodate your tardy visitor? Only people who are deluded about time choose the latter.

Of course, many of the choices in the workplace are not as clear-cut as this example. Sometimes the time bandits in our lives are hard to detect.

For example, we have an executive in one of our overseas offices who is extremely effective. He's smart, brash, energetic, and can close a deal as quickly as anyone. Most people misinterpret his frenetic pace and dynamic style to mean that he is someone who is very efficient with time. I've learned that is not true. He also has a strong independent streak, which compels him to flout many of the standard operating procedures in our company. If I send him a fax (which still conveys some sense of urgency to most people), there's no guarantee that he will respond to it in a timely manner. If I resend it three more times, he still may ignore it. In a way, he is a classic time bandit. People could waste weeks waiting for him to help them out. The only way to get his attention is by telephone.

At some point, I decided to yield to his peculiar style. I always call (and I've warned everyone in the company to do the same). If nothing else, it cuts down on all the futile time waiting to hear from him. I suppose I could urge him to mend his ways or punish him. But that would be a waste of time for both of us. And I would still be his victim.

UNDERSTAND YOUR EMPLOYEES' SENSE OF TIME

A few years ago I asked one of our sales executives to take on some additional responsibilities in the Far East. The sales executive was enthusiastic about the additional work, in part because he perceived it as a definite career boost.

His boss, however, was resisting the idea. "To do the job right," he argued, "will take at least 30 percent of his time. And I can't afford to lose 30 percent of him. It's not fair to me or my division."

On the surface, this division chief had a compelling argument. It was made even more compelling by the use of a specific percentage of time.

But the more I thought about it, the more I realized that there were at least three fallacies in his argument that were doing a disservice both to the employee and our company.

FALLACY #1: TIME IS NOT A ZERO-SUM GAME.

The biggest fallacy is that the argument treats an employee's time as if it were a zero-sum game—i.e., a gain of 30 percent in one area entails a corresponding loss of 30 percent in another. It presumes that an employee's work hours are finite and unyielding—say, forty hours a week—and that additional responsibilities mean an invasion into that forty hours.

In reality, the time people devote to work is extremely flexible. Although there are only twenty-four hours in a day and 168 hours in a week, employees have options about how many of those hours they spend at work. A lot of these options are determined by how motivated they are about their work. If an employee hates his job, he'll spend the minimum forty hours a week at it. If an employee is enthusiastic about the job, he may expand his time at work to fifty, sixty, or more hours a week.

What our division chief failed to recognize was that this sales executive was extremely enthusiastic about the new responsibilities. Because he saw the new job as a "promotion," he would make the time to do it right. He would pile the work on to what he was already doing rather than cut into it. If he was working forty hours a week before, he would increase his hours at least 30 percent. I fail to see how the company or the employee loses by this arrangement.

FALLACY #2: WHO CAME UP WITH 30 PERCENT?

The argument also ignores the great variability in the time required for different people to do the same tasks. After all, it might take me two hours to explain something to a client, whereas a more articulate executive could cover the same ground in twenty minutes.

This raises the obvious question: How does the division chief know that the job will take 30 percent of his subordinate's time? Where did he come up with 30 percent?

Over the years, I've seen a lot of good ideas fall apart because managers cannot agree on what percentage of someone's time an idea requires. The argument is always the same. One executive floats the figure of 30 percent. That percentage hangs over the discussion like a black cloud. No one questions it. Everyone assumes that it's correct when, in actual fact, it could fluctuate up or down depending on who is chosen to implement the idea.

But the most dangerous aspect of this fallacy is that it confuses the criteria you should be using in making assignments to your employees. Instead of worrying about how much time an employee is spending on a project, you should be considering whether he is capable of using that time wisely and effectively. Talent, not trumped-up percentages of time, is usually the more accurate measure of whether the job will get done.

FALLACY #3: BOSSES KNOW BETTER THAN EMPLOYEES.

A third fallacy is that the argument ignores the employee's opinion—even though the employee might know better than anyone else whether he can handle the new job.

In this particular case we were dealing with an experienced sales executive who's not only well organized but ambitious. He's not going to accept the assignment unless he's reasonably confident he can succeed at it. Given all that, you know he's going to make the time to be a success.

Yet for some reason his boss believes he knows better.

You find this attitude quite often among bosses who haven't fully thought out all the elements of a job. In my experience, when people don't understand a job, they tend to overestimate the time required to do it.

I'm guilty of this. For example, I know nothing about carpentry. If I needed a dining room table built, I would have no idea if a carpenter needs one afternoon to build it or three months. Yet I would lean toward three months because of the carpenter's mystique and my ignorance.

Likewise in this case. An otherwise smart executive put too much weight on the element of time, underestimated his employee's abilities and motivation, ignored his employee's opinion, and, not surprisingly, came up with the wrong conclusion.

Voice Lessons for People Who Can't Sing Others' Praises

In theory, there shouldn't be much to say about handing out praise. It doesn't take a genius to extol someone's achievements or to realize that doing so always has a positive effect. Yet the world is filled with otherwise bright people who are absolute dolts at delivering praise. They don't know when to do it. They do it grudgingly. They do it in the wrong forum. They don't do it often enough. And if they do it, they ruin the effect by following it up with criticism.

The truth is, when it comes to singing other people's praises, few of us are Pavarotti. All of us could use voice lessons. On the next page are some thoughts on how to start out.

1. WHAT'S YOUR CRITICISM-TO-PRAISE RATIO?

Over the years I've known many executives who actually take more pleasure in firing an employee than in telling a colleague or subordinate that he or she is doing a great job. I'm not sure why it has to be that way.

Perhaps delivering praise is a psychological hurdle they can't jump over. They regard praise as a zero-sum game. They think there are only so many kind words to go around and that praising someone takes the spotlight off them and somehow diminishes them. (Actually, it has the opposite effect. Praising someone elevates you in that person's eyes. Just think how highly you thought of the last person who took the time to tell you what a good job you were doing.)

One mental exercise to get over this hurdle is what I call the criticism-to-praise ratio. For one day (or one week) keep track of how many times you criticize and praise people. If you're handing out far more criticism than praise, you're doing something wrong (or you need to hire new people!).

In my mind, I've always tried to maintain a 1-to-1 ratio of criticism to praise. If I see that I'm lashing out at employees far more often than I'm patting them on the back, I try hard to reverse the imbalance. I go out of my way to hand out valid praise. It not only makes our people feel better, it makes me feel good, too.

2. ARE YOU IN A PRAISE-INTENSIVE BUSINESS?

Some businesses are praise-intensive, some are praise-resistant.

Ray Cave, the former managing editor of *Time* magazine, once told me that he was always conscious of how well, how often, and to whom he handed out praise. In his job, he had no choice. For him, editing a weekly magazine was a marathon of value judgments. He was constantly having to decide whether the ideas, articles, photographs, illustrations, and layouts his people produced were good enough for the magazine. As a result, he constantly had to decide whether to praise or criticize his writers, photographers, and artists. In that sense, publishing a magazine is a praise-intensive field. Remembering to praise people wasn't a problem for Ray Cave; it was one of his chief responsibilities.

Other businesses don't make it so easy on a boss. They are praise-resistant. For example, I can see how in our company a manager can get confused or forgetful about praise. When we sell a sponsorship to a sports event, it's usually the result of a complicated team effort. Who deserves the applause for the success? The individual who thought up the event? The executive who set up the meeting with the sponsor? Or the salesperson who closed the deal? Or the staff people who implement the event and keep the sponsor happy? With so many people sharing the glory, it's not hard to see how a boss neglects to single out individuals for praise.

Take a look at your company. If it's praise-intensive, are you handing out praise for maximum effect? If it's praise-resistant, are you handing it out at all?

3. Praise is a Great Control Mechanism.

I once had a teacher who was a master of praise. She always encouraged me with kind words when I had the right answer in a class discussion and wrote effusive comments like "Great job!!!" on my quiz papers. It didn't take me long to form a very favorable impression of her. I thought she was a great teacher. After a few weeks of her adulation, there came a day when I wasn't prepared for class and flubbed a test. She chided me for my sloppy work. Although her criticism wasn't vicious, it stung me and I promised myself not to let it happen again.

Only later did I realize that her constant praise had made her a very influential force in that classroom. I had become addicted to her high opinion of me. When withheld that opinion, I worked even harder to win it back.

Without making it sound too Machiavellian, there are two lessons for managers here.

First, praise is addictive. People will always think more highly of you for thinking highly of them—and they will make an extraordinary effort to recapture that high opinion if and when you withhold it.

Second, praise is a great control mechanism for managers. A boss's critical comments are much more potent and effective if he or she has laid down a foundation of sincere praise. People who accept the nice things you say about them tend to be more receptive when your comments are not so nice.

4. PRETEND PRAISE IS MONEY.

A wise executive once told me that he liked to think of handing out praise as the same as handing out money to his employees. "I can't always pay our people as much as I'd like to, so I pretend that praise is money. Whenever I tell one of my people that they did a wonderful job," he said, "it's like giving them a $100 bonus. Sure, they can't spend it on something nice. But they bank the praise in their mind—and they feel better about me and our company."

That may be the most compelling argument for praise: It will help you hang on to talented people when your money can't.

YOU ARE WHAT YOU KEEP

A friend of mine has an organizational theory that goes under the rubric, "You Are What You Toss Out." He believes that the higher you are in the corporate food chain, the more freedom you have to toss out the various forms of paper that cross your desk.

In his scheme of things, executive assistants, secretaries, and clerks are at the bottom of the chain—because they are obliged to save every piece of paper that comes their way.

Junior executives are next—because they must read and respond to every document from their superiors. And they usually have to save these documents in case their superiors ask about them at some future date. They also have no one below them to whom they can delegate paperwork.

Middle managers are in an awkward position. On the one hand, they have paperwork assaulting them from all levels of the company. On the other, they have the authority to pass some of this paperwork to subordinates and peers. According to my friend's "You Are What You Toss" theory, middle management is the critical level where paperwork and organizational efficiency intersect. How a middle manager handles paper is a reliable indicator of how organized he is. "If a middle manager is well organized," he says, "he tends to toss out (or forward) more paper than he keeps. That tells me that he's focused, that he's clear about his priorities. If he's poorly organized, he tends to keep everything. He's not focused. He doesn't know what to throw away, so he saves it instead. Everything to him has the same priority, which means it has no priority at all."

Taken to its logical extreme, my friend's theory would suggest that CEOs toss out all the paper that crosses their desks. And indeed, there's some truth to this. I have visited the offices of hundreds of CEOs in my career, and a great deal of them function quite effectively in pristine, uncluttered, paperless realms. There's a phone on their desk and perhaps a notepad (along with the obligatory photographs, trinkets, and pen-and-pencil set), but rarely have I found them swamped with the piles of files and documents so commonly found on lesser executives' desks. That's one reason they're the boss. They know what to toss out.

My friend has a valid point about the relationship between rank and paperwork. However, as the title of this section indicates, I would put a slightly different spin on it. I think the first critical decision an executive must make about any document is whether or not it is worth keeping. To make that decision, you have to be very clear about what kind of documents are important to you, which ones are vital for your continuing success, and what sort of information you will need at a future date. To answer those questions, you have to have your priorities in order and give some serious thought to what you want to accomplish not just in the next hour or day but in the next week, month, and year. In other words, you have to be mentally organized. In that sense, *you are what you keep.*

For example, although I envy those CEOs who lead a totally paperless existence, I probably keep 10 percent of the paper directed at me. (Of course, that also means I jettison 90 percent of my paperwork, which strikes me as a healthy percentage.) I can do this because years ago I analyzed how I work and how our company operates and I came to the conclusion that the documents that are worth keeping fall into three categories:

1. *I keep any document in which one of our executives promises to do something.* If an executive writes me a memo that, in effect, says, "Mark, I have an idea. It will cost the company x dollars in Year One. But I guarantee that it will return 5x dollars in Year Three. . . ." I will keep that memo in that executive's file. I've learned that, when it comes to promises, people tend to have very short memories, particularly when their promises don't pan out. But keeping that sort of memo is one of the most valuable management tools I have. In two or three years, when nothing has come of the idea, or it has failed, or it has proven to be only marginally profitable, I can always retrieve the memo and ask the executive, "What ever happened to this?" It's good to remind people that while they may forget a promise, I haven't.

2. *I hold on to any document that indicates a potential or ongoing conflict between employees or departments.* As a general rule, I usually don't have to keep this document too long—because I try to resolve the conflict quickly. But sometimes a quick solution isn't appropriate, so I will keep the document and return to it when the timing is more appropriate.

3. *I keep any document pertaining to a project or situation that is plagued by unresolved problems.* If there's a question mark hanging over the situation in the memo, I'd be a fool to let it slip from my grasp or hand it over to someone else. That piece of paper is usually my only reminder that a problem exists somewhere in our company and that I might need to act on it in the future.

I'm not sure what that system says about me—other than that I expect people to keep their promises, I don't like internal conflicts, and I worry about unresolved problems and don't worry about problems that have resolved themselves—but it suits my work habits and lets me feel that I am controlling my paperwork rather than it is controlling me.

What intrigues me about this "You Are What You Keep" theory is the fact that many executives never take the time to sit back every few years, look at their changing responsibilities and work habits, and make the necessary adjustments in how they deal with paperwork. As they rise in the organization, they forget to shed the junior executive mentality of saving every piece of paper. They continue to pore over and hoard every piece of paper—when in fact they should be throwing away more paper and keeping less.

If you're reading this in your office, stop reading now. Look around you. Are you comfortable with the volume of paperwork currently sitting on your desk? Has that volume increased or decreased in the last two or three years? Do you have a clear idea which documents on your desk you need to keep and which you don't? If not, isn't it time you thought about it?

McCormack's Rule of Worrying, or When to Leave Your Worries Alone

I once asked an associate to keep an eye on a pet project while I was out of the country. I knew the executive in charge of the project had a lot of things on his plate and I was worried that he would not follow up in precisely the manner we had planned or, worse, forget it completely.

The associate, who knew the executive well, told me my worry was misplaced. She said, "You don't have to get excited about this project because he's excited about it. What you have to worry about are all the things that don't excite him."

I thought that was a perceptive comment. It spawned McCormack's Rule of Worrying, which says, "You don't need two people worrying about the same thing at the same company. One is enough."

That's a handy guideline for any manager who isn't sure what he should be paying attention to and what he can leave alone. If someone else is worrying about a situation, you're covered. Worry about the things that everyone else is ignoring. I'd be hard pressed to come up with a simpler system for saving time, delegating shrewdly, and reducing stress.

Of course, it helps if you can size up what worries or excites your colleagues and what doesn't. I suspect this is one area where many of us overestimate how insightful we really are.

Try the following experiment:

Take a few moments to analyze what really excites your closest associate at work. Then write down what you think are his or her five biggest professional priorities. Then ask this associate to write down his or her own priority list. I'd be amazed if the two lists had three items in common. (A more basic, and potentially scarier, version of this experiment: List the five items you think each of your subordinates is working on. Then compare with your subordinates' versions. Again, I doubt if the lists come close to matching.) That's how negligent or unaware most of us are about what's really going on in our colleagues' minds.

I learned this some time ago with my assistant in London. Every executive has certain expectations of a personal assistant in terms of organization, follow-through, handling of correspondence, dealing with appointments, maintaining useful files, etc. This assistant was fully capable in these areas. But it took me years to realize that what really excited her was anything that had to do with travel and entertainment. She loved dealing with hotels and airlines, bargaining for better deals not only for me but for the entire company. She loved arranging my business luncheons and dinners—to the point where she would ask me in June what I wanted served at a luncheon for eight people on October 8. She excelled in this area in large part because it excited her.

If a stranger asked her, "What's this McCormack fellow do all day?" I honestly think that dining in restaurants, staying in nice hotels, and flying on airplanes would be near the top of her list. Forget about managing clients, growing the business, selling our company's services, and meeting a burgeoning payroll.

Her fascination with these areas inevitably cost her a little in other areas of her job. But I learned to deal with it. I never worried or second-guessed her about anything having to do with my travel and business entertaining—because I knew she would always have even the most complicated arrangements under control. (This saved me hours each month.) Instead, I worried about the tasks that didn't excite her as much. As I say, two people shouldn't worry about the same thing. One is enough.

Since then I've learned to keep a mental checklist of the concepts that excite the thirty or forty executives at our company whom I talk to regularly. It's not a big chore. I know executives who consistently lead off every phone conversation by reporting on the same single project. It doesn't take a genius to figure out that this is the one item on their plate that really excites them. Likewise, I deal with executives who cannot get through any discussion without mentioning a particular client or deal. Again, it's easy to see what turns them on.

Noticing these things is a great timesaver in that it dramatically reduces the number of things I have to worry about. I also suspect it saves a lot of wear and tear on employees. One of the biggest reasons employees lose faith in their bosses is that bosses nag them about things they don't need to be nagged about. If nothing else, at least I'm not hounding people for the wrong reasons.

The only time I worry about people's priorities is when they're in direct conflict with the company's priorities. We've had executives who, with some justification, take pride in a sports marketing concept they created. Unfortunately, that sort of pride is hard to contain sometimes. It compels them to force-feed their pet concept into any and every sales situation. If a customer wants to get involved in sports, the first thing out of their mouth will be the pet concept on the top of their mind, regardless of whether it's appropriate or the customer is clearly interested in something else we have to offer.

When an executive's excitement misses the bigger picture, I start to worry—alone.

• • •

THE McCORMACK RULES

- People who learn from their mistakes tend to have ability on the job. The ones who don't have a learning disability.

- Be ruthless about one thing, not everything.

- Delving deeply into one problem area is better than skimming halfheartedly over a half dozen areas.

- A sense of humor is never more valuable than in those dark moments in business when everyone is under intense pressure.

- The most fertile breeding grounds for bureaucracies are internal policies.

- Eternal vigilance is the only answer to controlling a bureaucracy.

- One of the toughest problems of being an entrepreneur is knowing what your core business is— and being sufficiently disciplined so you never lose sight of the core business as you try to grow your company and head off into more profitable areas.

- The only reason to draw an organizational chart is to help you decide which layers to eliminate.

- People work harder for the company's benefit when they only have to worry about what the person in the number one slot thinks.

- If people are curious about your company, don't tell them who you work for or how you're organized. Tell them what you actually do.

- If you have a good idea, you can usually improve its chances of coming to life if you can convince someone else that it's their idea as well.

- If you don't have credibility to keep a good idea moving forward, find a third party who does.

- Giving people deadlines to do something is one step shy of saying, "Do it!" It's not subtle, but it's persuasive.

- Give people room to err—but not twice.

- Everything else being equal, speed slaughters the competition.

- You can't expect to have a fast, nimble organization if you aren't fast and nimble yourself—and constantly striving to get faster.

- Any change in a personal relationship should be done with measured care rather than haste.

- People tend to be optimistic rather than pessimistic about how much they can accomplish in a day— and it usually costs them.

- When it comes to singing other people's praises, all of us could use voice lessons.

- Go out of your way to hand out valid praise. It not only makes your people feel better, it makes you feel good, too.

- People who accept the nice things you say about them tend to be more receptive when your comments are not so nice.

- The most compelling argument for being generous with praise is that it will help you hang on to talented people when your money can't.

- How a middle manager handles paper is a reliable indicator of how organized he is.

- The first critical decision an executive must make about any document is whether or not it is worth keeping.

- Keep any document in which one of your executives promises to do something. It's good to remind people that while they may forget a promise, you haven't.

- You don't need two people worrying about the same thing at the same company. One is enough.

- One of the biggest reasons employees lose faith in their bosses is that bosses nag them about things they don't need to be nagged about.

CHAPTER 3

How to Acquire and Maintain Authority

John Keegan, the British military historian, believes that great battlefield commanders such as Alexander the Great and Ulysses S. Grant possess five essential attributes of leadership:

- They show the troops they care.

- They tell the troops exactly what they want.

- They convince the troops they'll be rewarded if they fight, punished if they don't.

- They know when to attack.

- They share in their troops' danger.

At the risk of making business sound too much like warfare, I think Keegan has a point for any manager who aspires to be a leader. Here's how Keegan's five attributes can apply in business:

1. YOU HAVE TO PERSUADE THE TROOPS THAT YOU CARE ABOUT THEM.

This requires action rather than words, in the form of a personal gesture that treats people as human beings rather than revenue producers.

On one level this could mean permitting a valuable executive to take a vacation at the company's expense, or bring a spouse along on a business trip, or borrow your ocean-front condominium for the weekend.

On another level it means unwavering loyalty, even when it runs counter to economic common sense. I remember a few years ago when a CEO I know was going through a downsizing crisis at his company. The hungry young executives on his staff were urging him to get rid of several executives who had been with him for twenty years. Their best years were behind them, argued the Young Turks, and their salaries could be used better elsewhere.

The CEO knew they were probably right. But he couldn't bring himself to abandon associates who had been loyal to him for so many years. He kept them on and rode out the down cycle.

I believe he grew, rather than shrunk, as a leader in the eyes of his Young Turks for this gesture.

2. YOU HAVE TO BE ABLE TO TELL PEOPLE EXACTLY WHAT YOU WANT.

A leader will give his employees the big picture, saying, "This is where we'll be in five years."

A more effective leader will also mention the little details. Clear details, not "vision," are what employees carry with them from day to day.

For example, some years ago I suggested that our golf division consider signing up a relatively unknown golfer named Dave Martz the year Martz *didn't* win the American tour's long-driving contest. His drives were very long but crooked. But I believed people at exhibitions and corporate outings would love to watch him just hit the ball.

That's a very small detail in our golf division's overall scheme, yet bringing it up, I think, makes more of an impression about how much I care than a dozen of my lectures about the big picture. And it conveys exactly what I want.

3. YOU HAVE TO CONVINCE EMPLOYEES THAT THEY WILL BE REWARDED IF THEY FIGHT AND PUNISHED IF THEY DON'T.

In military life, this means honors and decorations for exceptional conduct.

In corporate life, it means titles and compensation (or the denial thereof) and the feeling that they're being meted out with consistency and fairness.

The most effective leaders rarely surprise their employees with promotions or demotions. They are constantly reminding them what's expected of them and how they're doing. There's nothing more counterproductive and cruel than letting someone go through the year thinking they're doing a great job when you actually think they're failing.

4. YOU HAVE TO KNOW WHEN TO ATTACK.

In business, this means timing: When do you take a soft or hard line, when do you become aggressive or passive, when do you really pay attention and when is it better to relax?

The surest sign of a leader is his or her ability to say, "Do it now!" and it gets done.

Knowing when to attack is also the easiest leadership quality to detect in junior employees. Few things catch my attention more quickly than a forceful memo from a lieutenant urging us to attack a flank now. If I agree and we win the battle, that lieutenant will soon be a captain.

5. YOU HAVE TO SHOW THE TROOPS THAT YOU SHARE THEIR DANGERS.

In military terms, this means being present on the battlefield. In business, this means leading by example.

Have you ever noticed how the most respected bosses are those who can do every job in the company—from the warehouse to the executive suite—and are not afraid to show it? That ability to get their hands dirty, to not only impose risk but to take it on themselves, is the source of their authority.

One of the more fortuitous things I did in the early years of our business was to bring along one of our executives to a meeting with the Simmons Mattress Co. and walk out with our first consulting contract.

I think that first example—where I could literally show an associate that you can walk into someone's office, ask for the order, and come out with a deal—is one reason that ex-ecutive has obtained so many contracts since.

IF YOU WANT DEFINITIVE ANSWERS, ASK DEFINITIVE QUESTIONS

I was wrapping up a sales call at an old friend's office recently when, for no apparent reason, his attention began to fade and he became visibly tense. I asked him if he felt all right.

He said, "I'm about to go into our monthly group meeting with the CEO. No matter how prepared I am, these meetings are always tense. The CEO has a talent for asking really tough questions that border on the sadistic."

Intrigued, I asked what made these questions so tough.

He said, "He can spot the tiniest flaw in any argument and then he'll zero in on it and pick it apart. And he poses questions that put everyone on the spot. I'll never forget the time I was pushing to get a promotion for a young man in my division who had been in the same spot for nine years. The CEO said, 'Nine years is a long time. Just tell me one thing. If this fellow applied for his current job today, with all that's happened in the last nine years, would you hire him on the spot? Or would you want to look at other candidates?' I have to admit, that caught me by surprise. Until then, it never occurred to me to question any promotion from within the ranks. It also forced me to back down from my ringing endorsement of the young man, which I suppose is what the CEO expected all along."

I can see why this CEO makes people nervous. He asks questions that require definitive answers. Those are the toughest questions—and most people aren't used to hearing them.

Most of the supposedly tough questions we face each day provide us with enough slack to wriggle out unharmed. Even a seemingly direct attack such as, "Why did you miss your sales quota this quarter?" has an escape hatch built into it. We can cite external forces beyond our control (*e.g.*, a trucker's strike delayed deliveries or reduced inventory). We can cite internal problems (*e.g.*, the marketing department didn't provide the supporting materials to promote the line). We can even blame a slowdown in the economy.

A tough boss might follow up with more tough questions: "Why didn't you anticipate the strike?" "Why didn't you tell me marketing was dropping the ball?" But in my experience, few bosses will push the questions much further than that. It's rude and intrusive. It sounds too much like an interrogation. Taken to its logical extreme, it forces the employee to admit in a public forum that he messed up—which is a fact that everyone in the room tacitly acknowledges but keeps to himself.

What's interesting here is how my friend's CEO has managed to ask the tough questions, to put people in a corner with no room to wriggle free, without appearing rude or belligerent.

I'm not a linguist or a professor of rhetoric, but it seems to me that when a boss asks why you didn't do something, in effect he's saying "You were wrong!" or "You messed up!" In my experience, these accusatory questions rarely elicit productive responses.

If you dissect the CEO's "Would you hire this man to-day?" question, you can see that he's not doing that. In posing a hypothetical situation, he's moving the discussion a step or two from reality. To most people, that's a safe, nonthreatening distance. It increases their comfort level. At the same time, the CEO has eliminated the prosecutorial tone from the discussion. He's not asking, "Why did you. . . ?" but rather "Would you. . . ?" It's a subtle difference, but it tends to make people more forthcoming.

Yet, in taking the hypothetical to its logical extreme ("Would you hire this man today?"), he's forcing his people to give an extreme answer, to give a definitive yes or no, to make an unambiguous commitment. Most questions in the work-place don't do that.

Ironically, the tough-sounding questions in business, the ones that say "You were wrong," are really the easy ones, be-cause they invariably let people off the hook. When some-one asks, "Why didn't you do this or that?" all you have to say is, "I messed up. I won't let it happen again." That's not a productive answer. It's just a mea culpa—an admission of guilt that usually goes unpunished.

The really tough questions are the ones that force people to take a stand. That's why the CEO above makes people squirm. He's constantly forcing them to state their position—and many people are not comfortable with that.

Once you appreciate this CEO's interrogative style, you'll see that it has broad applications in any managerial situation. I've used a variation in meetings with our executives. When people report on a recent sale, I sometimes ask them what they think a competitor across town would have generated in the same situation. It's not confrontational. It doesn't accuse them of leaving money on the table. It merely forces them to admit (to me and to themselves) whether they have done everything possible to maximize the opportunity.

Another variation on the same theme: In strategy meetings, I will sometimes ask our people, "What do you most fear our competition will do next?" Tossing that hypothetical into the air doesn't threaten people, but it does force them to think aggressively. A frank discussion about what our rivals should be doing inevitably leads to the question, "Why aren't we doing this ourselves?"

The same questioning technique can be used on existing or prospective clients. Because I know how complacency can creep into long-term customer relationships, I've sometimes sought meetings with a customer simply to pose the following question: "What would it take for our competition to lure you away?" It's not that I'm afraid the customer will jump ship. But there's some benefit to letting customers know on a regular basis that you don't take them for granted. There's also tremendous benefit to getting an answer to the "What would it take. . . ?" question. A customer who tells you what it would take to make him leave you is also telling you what it takes to make him stay.

How Much Information Do Employees Need to Know?

In the long run, it always pays to be as open as possible with employees. The problem for many managers is how you actually do it. Do you open your books to everyone? Do you share sensitive financial data only with a select few? Do you reveal such data in formal meetings, memoranda, or private discussions?

There's no single correct way to share data with employees. You can do it in any forum—and should. The key is to convince your employees that you are being as open with them as you can without damaging the business or giving away too much to the competition.

In my mind, the mechanics of sharing information are guided by one factor: the hierarchy of the organization.

You start out revealing minimal information at the lowest levels of the company and as you rise through the hierarchy you get more specific and revealing.

The secretary who just got hired should certainly hear the sentence, "This year is not going to be as good as 1995." She should hear that because there's nothing confidential about it and she should have a general idea about how the company is faring in a tough economy.

The next level up would be that secretary's boss who works in the same department. At this level, you tell people general information about the company, laced with specifics about their division: "The division grew 22 percent in 1995 but will only grow 8 percent in 1996, whereas expenses have increased from 10 percent last year to 22 percent in 1996." At the next level, where you have people running departments, you broaden their exposure to classified information. You not only include them on all the data about how their department is doing, but you place those numbers in a larger context—by comparing those numbers against other departments and discussing how the entire division has performed. You not only talk numbers ("Division income went up from $900,000 to $1.1 million, but expenses increased from $870,000 to $1.35 million. . ."), but you delve into why expenses are outpacing income ("We opened a new office, hired two more executives. . .").

These people's bosses would get even more information. The higher you go, the more specific information you get and the more access you have not only to information about your specific area but about the whole company.

Remembering the hierarchy is basically all a manager needs to know about sharing vital information.

The more isolated an individual is within a particular sector of the company, the more important it is for them to have access to all the numbers relevant to them. But that doesn't mean they need to know all the numbers that everyone else is getting.

If someone in our company works on golf events in Europe, it's crucial that he knows all the financial and legal information about golf in Europe. It's also generally important that he has a feel for how the company is doing. But it's not important that he knows the corresponding data for, say, our tennis or equestrian events. Knowing those facts has no impact on his job, his performance, or his career. He's better off being out of the loop until his superiors feel he has a need to know.

I'm not sure everyone will agree with my thinking on this. But I run a private company that handles the financial, legal, and personal details of many well-known individuals. My worst nightmare is seeing some confidential data made public against a client's wishes, because I shared more rather than less information with my employees.

THE "GUN TO THE HEAD" SOLUTION

In a management meeting at our company not long ago, one of our executives was bemoaning the fact that he couldn't get anyone else in the company interested in supporting his group's projects. He felt he was out there on the fringes, working alone, while many of his colleagues were benefiting from our tradition of cooperation and teamwork.

I sympathized with him. One of our company's more worrisome phenomena is that our executives tend to perform heroically only when the company's money is at risk.

I noticed this a few years ago when we became the marketing agents of the men's professional tennis tour around the world. We had guaranteed the Association of Tennis Professionals (ATP), which runs the tour, more than $50 million to do so. It was amazing how this multimillion-dollar guarantee motivated people in all corners of the company, not just in the tennis division. We didn't come up with the guarantee off the top of our heads. Nevertheless, the company was on the hook for a major chunk of money. If we weren't creative and aggressive about exploiting every commercial opportunity associated with men's tennis—not just the obvious big-ticket items such as television rights and tour sponsorships—we would fall short of the guarantee. That shortfall would affect the company's profits, which in turn would affect everyone's compensation.

The good news is that our people performed beyond expectations. We covered our exposure with room to spare.

The bad news, at least from my perspective as a manager, is that we sometimes have to hold a gun to people's heads to

make things happen. As I say, this is a worrisome phenome-
non. And I'm sure it is not unique to our company.

If a restauranteur decides to spend $250,000 to expand his
restaurant, it should be obvious to everyone on the staff that
they'll need more patrons to fill the extra tables. If they don't,
there won't be enough money for Christmas bonuses. Thus,
everyone from the chef to the busboys makes a greater effort
to be nice to diners. People should give that extra effort no
matter what, but they tend to volunteer it only when they realize the owner's money and, consequently, their paycheck
are on the line.

Indifference and sloth aren't the only reasons people need
a gun to the head to get motivated. At our company, the culprit is usually the fact that our people and projects are so widely
dispersed in so many areas. A team of executives will go to a
meeting and float a dozen new golf ideas or twenty publishing
ideas in front of a potential customer. Everyone leaves the meeting. Then, nothing happens with those ideas—because (a) no
single individual is being held accountable for the success or failure of these trial balloons and (b) the company hasn't lost
anything if the idea doesn't come to fruition. It's incremental,
nice-to-have income, the kind that keeps a company growing.
Unless the customer buys into one of the ideas at that first
meeting, there's nothing spurring our people to follow up and
continue selling. Each of the executives at that meeting has
plenty of ongoing projects demanding his or her attention. But
the moment top management says, "OK, we have a lot of money
riding on this concept," and people feel their paycheck is
threatened, that's when it grabs everyone's attention.

Unfortunately, you can't bet the ranch on every concept.
Nor can you constantly exhort the troops to make everything

top priority. Not everything deserves a high priority, and after a while they'll tune you out. Effective managers must find more subtle ways to manufacture a sense of urgency in their organizations. They know that if they constantly have to put the figurative gun to people's heads, at some point they'll have to pull the trigger. Here are four less violent methods to achieve the same result.

1. FIND A CORPORATE MANTRA.

Quite early in his post as chairman of General Electric, Jack Welch came up with what may be the all-time most effective and most quotable management mantra for instilling a sense of urgency within an organization. He declared that *GE would sell off or get out of any business where it couldn't be the number one or two market leader.* If executives up and down the GE hierarchy ever thought they had the luxury of letting a money-losing division slowly find its niche, Welch's edict ended that. It's the clearest statement of a fact that all managers know in their bones: It's tough to make money if you're running third, fourth, or fifth in your field.

The GE corporate mantra may not make sense for every business, but I can't think of a better way to get people to focus on things that matter.

2. FIND A WINDOW OF OPPORTUNITY, THEN CLOSE IT.

In our business, the windows of opportunity open and close with dazzling rapidity. An athlete does something extraordinary, such as winning a Grand Slam tournament, and we have only a finite amount of time to capitalize on that success. Next week, next month, or next year some other athlete may do something extraordinary, and our client becomes old news. It's a fickle business. You'd think everyone would appreciate that. Yet I constantly have to remind people to seize the moment.

It's not that people don't know that it's much easier to sell a "hot" client. But they sometimes forget how quickly clients can cool off. They think the heat will last forever. That's one reason I almost always attach a deadline to any marketing blitzes we attempt for a client. A rising star who has just won Wimbledon in July is more marketable than the same star who has just lost the U.S. Open in September. We should be selling hard in the two months in between.

Once you've shown your people that the window of opportunity is open, then also threaten to close it.

3. FORM A TEAM, NOT A COMMITTEE.

Not everyone responds to threats or motivational talks or deadlines. But everyone notices when you start throwing a lot of manpower at a troubled division or project. Moving people out of their traditional roles and concentrating them in one spot instantly increases the urgency of the situation. It means you're making an investment of company resources—and that you expect a return on that investment. If you're clever about the rank and stature of the people you redeploy, the investment is not much of a gamble.

Some years ago it was obvious to me that the outdated state of our Cleveland accounting had reached crisis proportions. I could have let our accounting people solve the problem. I could even have given them a deadline. But this was a crisis, not a problem. And I wanted everyone to realize this. So I formed a team, a mix of senior and mid-level people from other parts of the company, and had them stop whatever they were working on. This wasn't a committee that would meet once a month. This was a SWAT team dedicated to one task. One of the executives was, in effect, transferred from London to Cleveland for the duration. I suspect that telling senior people to drop what they're doing and moving them to Cleveland was one way to suggest the urgency of the crisis. I also suspect it was a major factor in how quickly the team got us back on track.

4. SET AN "IMPOSSIBLE" PERFORMANCE STANDARD.

It's hard to believe that there was a time when there was no company called Federal Express promising to deliver a package by 10:30 A.M. the next day. But overnight delivery is the kind of "impossible" performance standard that soon becomes standard operating procedure.

Rubbermaid has an internal goal of developing a new product a day. That's 365 new products a year in the allegedly mundane world of housewares. That may be an impossible standard for other companies to emulate because few of them even bother to set any sort of performance standard. But Rubbermaid's people have risen to the challenge every year.

I don't know why this surprises people. If the staff is projecting 5 percent growth, even the fairest, most forgiving CEO will automatically double it and push for 10 percent. The CEO knows that the staff is setting the bar at a height they can clear. It's his job to get them jumping a little higher.

That's the beauty of setting so-called impossible standards. You don't have to put a gun to someone's head to make them jump. Just set the bar a little higher than before, and your best people will rise to the occasion.

The "This Hurts Me More Than It Hurts You" Syndrome

I once asked a longtime friend how his daughter, a recent college graduate, was doing. The father explained that she had landed a job at a great company but she was having tremendous problems getting along with her boss.

This information didn't make much of an impression on me until a few days later when I had the same conversation with another couple. Their son (a recent graduate) had also found a dream job that was turning into a nightmare because of the way his boss was treating him.

I shouldn't have been surprised. I've always thought that one of the toughest transitions to make in a career occurs right at the start of the career, when you are just out of school and ready to conquer the world. The problem isn't youth or inexperience or grandiose ambition. The big problem is *authority figures*. How to deal with authority figures (*i.e.*, bosses) is just one of the many things they don't teach you at Harvard Business School, or any other institution of higher learning. But they should.

It's easy to see why these two bright young people (and many more like them) were having problems with their new bosses. That's the way they were trained. For the first two decades of their lives, every authority figure they'd dealt with had been someone who had their best interests at heart.

A wag I know calls this the "This Hurts Me More Than It Hurts You" syndrome. That's the line parents use when they are punishing their child for some unpardonable act of negligence or disobedience. They're punishing the child for his or her own good, so the child won't repeat the error. It's a learning experience.

Young people face the same instructional dynamic with virtually every authority figure in their lives from nursery to graduate school.

A teacher who knows they are not living up to their potential tells them, "It kills me to give you a bad grade, but that's the only way to teach you not to hand in shoddy work."

A coach suspends a star player for missing practice. The suspension hurts the coach and the team, but the overriding objective is to teach the player a lesson about discipline.

Each of these authority figures—parent, teacher, coach— is looking out for the young person's best interests.

All that changes when they enter the workplace. Suddenly they're working for a boss who doesn't necessarily have their best interests at heart. This new authority figure in their life is looking out primarily for himself.

That's a dramatic transition for a lot of young people, especially if they don't recognize the change they're going through. The sting of being berated or punished by a boss is no longer softened by the implicit understanding that "this hurts me more than it hurts you." The truth is, it doesn't hurt the boss at all!

Fresh-faced youngsters straight out of college aren't the only ones who experience this rude awakening. It happens when people switch jobs. If you leave a paternalistic company where everyone treats you like "family" to work for a hard-boiled, every-man-for-himself organization, you might have problems with your new superiors, especially if you don't appreciate the different styles.

There's a managerial irony here, too. I realize the current "lean and mean" management gospel promotes a corporate culture where bosses have to look out for their own best interests. When the daily themes being pounded into managers' heads are "cut the fat," "produce or perish," and "what have you done for me lately?" it's not hard to see why bosses are less empathetic and nurturing than our parents, teachers, and coaches.

But here's the rub: Despite all the economic pressures that currently favor the cold, heartless boss who never loses sight of the bottom line, I still think managers are better off if they model themselves on parents, teachers, and coaches. In the long run, a company where the authority figures have the employees' best interests at heart (and the employees know that) will outlive a company where they don't.

It's easy to pay lip service to this noble sentiment. It's tougher to practice it. Let's say I promote someone because he has a big account in his pocket. I give him a hefty salary increase and an important title commensurate with the huge revenue he is adding to our coffers. Let's also say that a year after the promotion, he loses the account.

As a manager, I have two options here.

I can look out for my interests and those of the company. He's failed. So I punish him by cutting his salary, giving someone else his fancy title, and, if he loses another account, getting rid of him. In strict economic terms, that's the right thing to do. It's cold but it makes sense. No one can fault you for it.

Or I can put his interests ahead of mine. I can see that he's hurting and going through some bad times. If I care about him as a human being and support him when he's down, and if everyone in the company sees me doing that, then I've created more of a warm family feeling in the company. It makes people feel more secure. I'm behaving more like a parent than a boss. Carrying this employee until he gets his bearings again might cost the company some money in the short term, but you'll never convince me that this isn't the right approach.

THE DANGERS OF DELEGATING

It's commonly accepted wisdom that an effective, well-organized executive knows how to delegate tasks to subordinates. It's a simple equation: The more you can delegate, the more you can get done. Delegating not only makes you appear more commanding to your subordinates and more productive to your superiors, it's also liberating. While your delegatees are doing the onerous and time-consuming tasks, you are free to pursue new challenges and opportunities.

It's hard to argue with this. I happen to be a very aggressive delegator. I don't need the ego-gratification of doing everything by myself so I can say "I did this" and "I did that." I get a bigger kick out of being able to say, "I got someone else to do it." In my version of an ideal world, I would be able to delegate every request, every memo that crosses my desk, every routine responsibility to someone in our company, so I could spend my time thinking about new business ideas, maintaining business relationships, and calling on new prospects. Alas, I'm nowhere near achieving this ideal state—because there are forces at play in most organizations that can make delegating risky or frustrating.

1. BEWARE THE SUBCONTRACTOR.

The worst thing about delegating is when I delegate a job to someone and they, in turn, delegate it to someone else. In effect, they are "subcontracting" out the assignment.

The dynamic is a little like building a house. Unless you are a master at carpentry, masonry, electricity, plumbing, and the other building trades, you don't build a house by yourself. Instead, you hire a contractor who, in turn, hires subcontractors skilled at carpentry, masonry, plumbing, etc. You hire the contractor, in large part, on the basis of the quality of the subcontractors he deals with and on his ability to get them to do quality work on budget and on time. There's some risk involved, because you have to trust the contractor's choice of subcontractors.

But there's one crucial difference in an office environment. When you build a house, you *expect* the contractor to delegate most of the work. When you delegate a task to someone in your company, (a) you don't expect them to "subcontract" it to someone else and (b) they rarely tell you that they did it. I find that frustrating and counterproductive.

For example, not long ago I asked one of our golf executives to find out how much money we could expect for a client's golf instructional book in France, Germany, and Scandinavia. We have publishing people in our company who specialize in golf books and know the international market for such books. But I specifically asked this executive because I knew our golf book specialist was busy on another project and (as a CEO who's always looking for executive talent) I was curious to see how he would handle the assignment.

Unfortunately, he turned over the job to our golf book specialist, who a few weeks later gave him a dollar figure for each of the three territories. He then wrote me a brief memo, without mentioning the golf book specialist, in which he summarized the dollar totals.

When I followed up to ask him which German publishers were interested in the book, he couldn't answer the question. He wasn't the one who had researched the marketplace. Therefore, he wasn't knowledgeable. The best he could do was refer me to our golf book specialist. That's frustrating. If I had wanted our specialist to do the job, I would have asked him originally.

To me, this is a delegator's worst-case scenario because it wasted everyone's time and I didn't learn everything I wanted to know.

Perhaps more frustrating, though, is how it cancels out my skill as a delegator. I don't delegate lightly. I give a lot of thought to which person in our company I want to do a specific job. When that person passes it on to someone else without letting me know, in effect he is minimizing my thinking on the subject. He's saying he knows better than I do—and that is not always the case.

2. BEWARE THE BOUNCE-BACK.

Another insidious feature of delegating is the bounce-back.

When you delegate a task to someone, you are basically sweeping that chore off your desk and onto someone else's desk. You don't expect it to return to your desk until the job is 100 percent done.

Unfortunately, there are people in every organization who can't resist pushing the chore back onto your desk before it is completed.

Some people, out of laziness or insufficient ability, only do half the job and bounce it back to you in the fond hope that you will forgive them and do the rest yourself.

Then there are people who insist on constantly updating you on how they're doing with the assignment. When they get 20 percent done, they give you a progress report. Then they report again at 50 percent and 80 percent. The job keeps bouncing back to you. When they complete the task, they expect a standing ovation and your eternal gratitude.

Either way, both types are defeating the essential purpose of delegating—which is to transfer the problem from your mind to theirs.

It only takes one or two assignments to identify these masters of the bounce-back. If you keep delegating to them, you have only yourself to blame.

3. BEWARE MISINTERPRETATIONS.

In delegating tasks, you also run the risk that your requests will be misinterpreted. An assignment that is intended to simplify your life often ends up complicating the lives of everyone around you.

A few years ago, while my wife Betsy Nagelsen was preparing to play at Wimbledon, she mentioned that she would like to find some grass-court tennis shoes to wear at the tournament. I passed this on to my long-time London assistant, Sarah Wooldridge.

Sarah asked, "What brand?"

I told her, "Puma."

"What specific model?"

I said, "I think Betsy liked a pair that Sylvia Hanika wore at the pre-Wimbledon tune-up tournament at Eastbourne."

So Sarah relayed this information to our tennis division: "Betsy wants the grass-court shoes from Puma that Sylvia Hanika wore at Eastbourne."

Now, because it was coming from me and my wife was involved and Sarah is very persistent, this simple request got magnified by a factor of ten by our tennis division. It filtered through the many layers of our European operations until someone in our Munich office contacted Sylvia Hanika's manager and finally reached Hanika herself. Of course, by then the oft-repeated request had been garbled into, "Betsy wants the shoes you wore at Eastbourne."

Four months later, while Betsy and I were in Los Angeles, she received a package containing Sylvia Hanika's used grass-court tennis shoes.

I suppose Betsy or I could have avoided all this simply by calling Hanika directly. In hindsight, this is probably the biggest danger of delegating. As it travels through the various layers of an organization, a simple request can get distorted to the point where it bears no likeness to the original request.

It's good to remember this. In our eagerness to delegate as much as we can, sometimes we're better off doing things ourselves.

"You Pack It, You Jump It," or the Parachute Principle

A young executive was complaining that his boss hardly paid attention to him and his activities at work. The complaint confused me for a moment. Ordinarily I'd congratulate the employee on his good fortune. Having a boss who leaves you alone is usually a blessing. It's practically a cause for celebration when you consider the alternative—*i.e.*, working for a micromanaging maniac who's constantly looking over your shoulder and second-guessing your results.

But the more I thought about the young man's predicament, the more I worried. Why was I paying his boss? Managers are *supposed* to pay attention to their staff. They're *supposed* to look over their employees' shoulders and second-guess their results. Ideally, managers should do this without irritating people. But given the choice between (a) people being left alone but missing their targets and (b) people feeling overmanaged but making their targets, I'll always choose the latter. I prefer our people know that someone is watching at all times. Paranoia (if it's healthy and benign) is a success skill. Neglect is not.

I had a chat about the young man's complaint with the manager in question. He had a fast response: "Look, I think I'm up to speed on most of the things he's working on. But I can't get mixed up in or even think about every idea he brings to me. If it's a bad idea and a waste of time, I kill it immediately.

"But if it's a promising idea, I operate on the 'Parachute Principle.' His idea is his parachute. You pack it. You jump it." Then he explained the Principle's advantages:

- Employees perform better with no interference. They're more creative when no one is tossing cold water on their hot ideas.

- On their own, they're practically forced to think like entre-preneurs. They're more willing to take risks.

- They don't have to share the credit. If they hit the target, they get all the applause.

It was a compelling argument. But this Parachute Principle has negatives, too:

- There's a fine line between "no interference" and "no guid-ance." And everyone in the workplace needs guidance, some more than others.

- People feel varying degrees of apprehension and self-doubt when the boss tells them, "You're on your own." Everyone needs support, some more than others.

- "You pack it, you jump it" is not exactly a vote of confidence for the idea or project. If it were, the boss would jump in, too.

- It stifles the development of a mentoring relationship between managers and their subordinates.

I don't think managers ever get a perfect handle on how often they should inject themselves into their employees' activities. It varies from employee to employee. But I do know that employees, knowingly or not, usually provide the answer.

We learned this from the client side of our business. Clients let you know loud and clear how much they want you involved. On the one hand, there are clients who want their managers in the mix on virtually every decision. They're the kind who will call from an airport counter because their reservation is lost, wanting to know, "What should I do?" There's nothing wrong with that. That's our job. But being aware of this makes it a lot easier to accept such a call.

Then there are clients who call us only during a major crisis or when they clearly feel out of their depth in a business situation. That's all right, too. Timely intervention is the essence of what a client manager does.

Intervention is also the essence of what all managers do.

As a rule, there are two occasions when managers need to intervene in their subordinates' activities: *before* the work begins and *after* it is well underway. Before is easily the more important of these two. That's when employees are literally telling their bosses that they need guidance, that they want their bosses involved.

For example, when an executive comes to me with a good idea that he or she wants to pursue, there are several levels to how I respond.

I could say, "Great idea. Run with it." That's the easiest thing in the world to do and the minimum level of involvement. I hope I don't have to think about the idea again.

I could say, "Run with it, but keep me informed." That's marginally more involvement.

I could say, "Before you run with it, show it to Tom and Susan and let me know what they think." That's slightly more caring still.

I could say, "Before you run with it, let *me* show this to Tom and Susan. I want to know what they think." That's even more involvement. I'm trying to make a contribution. I'm actually beginning to manage.

I could also say, "Let me help you on this." That's serious involvement on my part, and not always welcome. Intervention to one employee is interference to another. Better yet, I could phrase it as a question: "Do you want me to help you on this?" The answer tells me a lot about how much or how little I need to be involved. Whatever my response, the key is this: I'm thinking about my involvement at the earliest stages of a project, and I'm thinking about it from my employees' perspective as well as my own. That's my big gripe with the Parachute Principle. It's a disguise for managers who don't want to manage. It absolves them of responsibility at the moment when they need to be most responsible.

Although it's admirable to trust your employees and let them fail or succeed on their own, when employees come to you with an idea, they're not asking you only for a "green light" on the project. They're also seeking your seal of approval and your vote of confidence. They're testing your commitment. The various levels of intervention you employ before the work begins—from the uninvolved "You pack it, you jump it" to the seriously involved "Let me help you"—speak volumes about what you think of the idea.

It also usually determines how much you have to intervene after the work is underway. In my experience, the more commitment you display at the beginning of a project, the less involved you have to be at the end.

WHEN SOMEONE IS WORKING AGAINST YOU

A friend of mine, a division chief at a large broadcasting and publishing conglomerate, once told me a story about dealing with a difficult employee.

My friend had just been promoted into the top spot of the company's flagship publication, where he was in charge of more than a hundred writers, editors, and graphic artists. These people were extremely bright, creative, experienced, and (more than occasionally) quite temperamental. Managing them required patience, guile, and tact—the last of which was not my friend's strong suit.

After a few months on the job, my friend noticed that one of his editors was dawdling on completing a major editorial project. When my friend pointed out that he would like to see something in writing soon, the editor shrugged his shoulders and mumbled an unconvincing excuse. Finally, out of frustration, my friend decided to pull rank on the subordinate.

"You're going to do this," he said, "and the reason you will is because you work for me."

The editor replied, "I don't work for you. I work for the company. You just happen to be the human being the company has inserted as my current boss."

The editor was arguing semantics, perhaps. But as my friend thought about it later, it was an important distinction.

If a manager's authority rests on the fact that his loyal supporters work "for" him, then the flip side is also true: As a manager you will always have people who, for whatever reasons, resent or suspect you. They hold back their loyalty and support. If they're not for you, then they're against you.

My friend walked away from this mini-confrontation a much wiser manager.

As he explained it to me later, "A fellow who goes out of his way to tell you that he doesn't work for you is clearly telling you what he thinks of you. He is drawing a line. He's saying that working together is not going to be a genial, collegial exercise. It's not even going to be a case of constructive friction. It's going to be war."

Apparently, this editor was harboring deep envy over my friend's promotion and was having a tough time concealing it.

"The good news in all this," said my friend, "was that this fellow was also teaching me, wittingly or otherwise, how to deal with him. I could see that if I ever needed something from him, it would be a delicate situation. He would find a way to resist. I could order him to do it—but he would sabotage me because he didn't accept my authority.

"From then on, I knew that everything I asked of this editor would have to come through intermediaries or in such an oblique manner that he would think it was his idea."

That's an important thing to know about managing people. I think it's prudent for every manager to identify who among his troops he considers for or against him. Of course, unlike my friend's case, not every subordinate will tell you straight to your face whether he is your ally or adversary.

But they leave telltale clues about their loyalties in many ways:

- The way they describe their responsibilities;

- The job title they prefer ("assistant this" or "associate that" won't do for some adversaries);

- How scrupulously they keep you informed of their activities (or fail to);

- How proprietary they become when you interfere in their territory;

- How they introduce you in meetings or public forums. (Your loyalists, for example, won't have a problem admitting that you are their boss, that they work for you. They'll say as much to others. Your adversaries, on the other hand, may come up with euphemisms to get around that.)

The fact is, saying someone works for you is belittling to some people. It insults their dignity and sense of autonomy.

Perhaps the most prudent policy in employee relations is to eliminate the words *for* and *against* from your vocabulary. When I introduce an employee to outsiders, I always try to say this individual is working *with* me, even though it's clear to everyone present that this person is under my wing. It doesn't matter to me how I describe our people. Frankly, it doesn't make much of an impression on the outsiders. I do so only because it matters to the person I'm describing.

WHO'S READING YOUR MISSION STATEMENT?

An entrepreneur I know went away with his four partners for three days to come up with a corporate mission statement for his company. Now that the partners had 180 employees, they felt they needed one to keep the company on track. But after three days, the partners were no closer to a consensus about their company's "mission" than when they started.

"I guess there was some value in the session," he told me. "If nothing else, we learned how far apart we are on fundamental issues like management structure, financial goals, and our responsibility to our workers."

His remarks left me shaking my head. I always thought mission statements were supposed to be serious or sincere greeting cards that explain an organization's reason for being. What did that have to do with management structure and financial goals? Those items belong in a business plan or year-end review, not in a mission statement.

I suspect that's one reason my friend and his partners had such a tough time coming up with a noble statement justifying their existence: They weren't clear about what a mission statement is supposed to do.

I also suspect they weren't clear about who would be reading it. I always wonder for whom mission statements are really written. Is it people inside the company or people outside? I know one company whose sole employees are a husband and wife. Yet their letterhead is decorated with a mission statement containing some of the loftiest phrases about excellence, quality, and the primacy of the customer that I've ever heard. Who are they talking to? It can't be their workforce. After all, there are just the two of them; they'd be talking to themselves. It must be directed at their customers (which explains why they emblazon the statement on their stationery).

I'm not criticizing this couple for having a mission statement. (In fact, they are impressive people and their mission

statement only confirms what I already know about them—
that they are first-rate business people.) I mention this because
my friend's inability to reach a consensus with his partners may
simply be that he never appreciated Step One of any mission statement: Who's it for—your employees or your customers?

We don't have a mission statement at our company, but
if we did I'm sure the statement would differ depending on
whether it was for internal or external consumption.

Soon after my first *Harvard* book came out, a publisher approached me about writing a follow-up book. I was still en-
joying the success of the first book, so I wasn't really thinking
about the next book.

I asked the publisher, "What should I write about?"

"It should be about what really matters to you in business," he said.

After a few seconds of thought, I said, "What I really like
is making money from my ideas." Thus, "How to Make Money
From Your Ideas" became the rather blunt (and incredibly
bland) working title typed into the book contract.

If I had to write a mission statement for our people, I
don't think I could improve on "making money from ideas."
That statement speaks volumes about how highly I regard
profitability and *creativity*. Without profits, you don't stay in
business. Without creativity, you can't compete.

I like the brute simplicity of it. I also like all the noble
phrases that statement leaves out. There's no mention of our
commitment to excellence, or the empowerment of individuals, or our responsibility to our community, or our devotion
to our clients. To me, such lofty sentiments are givens. They
come with the territory. They are subsets of "making money

from ideas." You can't compete if you don't strive for excellence. You don't hold on to talented people if you don't empower them. And you don't keep clients happy if you don't come up with ideas that they would never have thought of without you.

Now, if I were composing a mission statement for external consumption, I doubt if "We like to make money from our ideas" would be a very palatable statement—at least not to our clients, customers, and employees.

I'm sure our clients would wonder where they fit in with our "mission." What are we doing to benefit them? In a personal services business such as ours, a good mission statement must recognize that our clients are our core business. Protecting and advancing their interests is Job One. To retain and recruit clients, we would need to broadcast that core principle somewhere in our mission statement.

Prospective customers might be put off by the self-serving nature of the statement. It would be hard to dispute the impression that we are promoting a "sell and walk" culture in which we feel we have achieved our goal once we take the customer's money. A proper statement would acknowledge somehow that we don't feel we have completed a sale until the customer is completely satisfied.

Finally, I think the statement willfully neglects the importance of our employees. If our people are, in fact, our biggest asset, we should tell that to the world and to our people. If a "mission statement" is an organization's license to brag about its standards and aspirations, then it ought to mention the assets and resources that back up that braggadocio. In our case (and, I suspect, in most organizations) the backup is our people.

DO YOU HAVE THE RIGHT PROFILE?

I'm always puzzled when I hear employees talk about a colleague who has a "hidden agenda." I'm puzzled because most people don't try too hard to conceal their agendas. How could they? When you come right down to it, employees basically have four agendas in the workplace. They either want:

- More money

- A better title

- More power

- A higher profile

The first three—title, money, power—are easy to comprehend. Profile is a little trickier to handle.

By profile I mean a person's visibility inside and outside the company. If an executive concludes a significant deal, does everyone in the company know about it immediately? (That's a high profile internally.) Or does he go about it quietly, immediately moving on to the next project? (That's low profile.) Is he quoted regularly in the media? (That's high profile externally.) Or is he content to remain a powerful force out of the public eye? (That's obviously low profile externally.)

I think profile is the trickiest agenda because, while most people are pretty clear about the kind of title, money, and power they seek, they're not as decisive about the kind of profile they want, nor are they very thoughtful about the rewards and consequences of achieving a certain profile.

As a manager I don't see anything wrong with having employees with a high profile in the industry or in their specialized area of expertise. In our company we have many executives who have gained a relatively high profile in their respective areas—everything from hockey to tennis to television to classical music. It's not surprising. These executives have very high-profile clients. It's natural that some of that visibility will rub off on the client's chief business adviser.

For the most part this is good. A high profile gives an executive credibility and a perception of authority as well as a little glamour. It can give him entree through certain doors that might otherwise be closed to him. Since high-profile people, by definition, are highly quotable, it also gives us easy access to the media where, if necessary, we can state or defend our position in the press. Also, having a high-profile executive on our team might strengthen our position in areas not directly related to that executive. I know instances where the fact that a high-profile executive running one of our U.S. operations has helped us in negotiations with international organizations, even though that U.S. executive may have nothing to do with the actual deal.

But there are risks. For one thing, if you have a high-profile executive running a division, there's the widespread perception that he or she *is* the division. There's no room for a second high profile in that division. That's risky for the company. If the division head gets run over by a truck, there should be a second-in-command ready to step into any existing relationships with almost the same authority and credibility. That's not likely if the division head has spent years grooming and polishing his own public profile at the expense of the company or his associates.

That's one reason I always urge our top managers to take along their top associate to major meetings. If something should happen to them, I want the relationship to be with our company, not with their high profile. As a manager you have to protect your company if you are giving an employee the chance to increase his profile.

One of the thorniest issues arises when there is a dramatic disparity between an employee's profile internally and externally. I remember some years ago when we assigned the day-to-day management of the very young Bjorn Borg to a junior executive in our company. When Borg became a superstar, this young executive ascended with him. Suddenly he had a very high profile as a superstar manager in the tennis community. He was always being quoted in the press. This dramatic improvement in stature dramatically increased his value in the marketplace.

Inside the company, though, he remained a relatively junior employee. We knew that anyone, even a wet-behind-the-ears novice, could make big deals for Borg when he was number one in the world. We also knew that managing Borg wasn't a one-man show, that our senior tennis people were providing much of the guidance behind Borg's career. In effect, we had created a monster. That's another area you have to sort out carefully: Sometimes high profiles are self-created; sometimes they're created by the company or simply by luck.

Ultimately we lost this young executive. Because of his high profile he received job offers that were far more generous than we thought he was worth. Good for him, not so good for us.

The most dangerous high profile, however, is the one at odds with the company's goals. We've had people in our company whose personal agenda is to be as invisible internally as possible. Few people know who they are, what they do, or where they may be at any given moment. By itself, there's nothing really wrong with that. There are lots of people who by temperament and inclination prefer to do their jobs in the background. (Our financial management executives fall into this category. They work in a fairly arcane area, managing money for well-known clients. But the fact that they're dealing with other people's money obligates them to operate at a very high level of confidentiality. In other words, it's their job to be low-profile.) The problems arise when people use that invisibility to shield themselves as they use the company's resources to build up a high profile outside the company.

As a manager, I've learned that a big disparity between an employee's internal and external profile is one of the surest signs of a rogue employee—that is, someone who is pursuing a personal agenda at company expense.

We once had an executive in our athletics division who fit this profile. She represented some of the world's best runners at a time when marathoning was at its commercial peak. This gave her a high profile within the international racing community. Inside the company she was barely a blip on the corporate radar, which apparently was how she liked it. The low profile internally freed her to cultivate a very high profile externally. She could do and spend whatever she pleased, because everyone was too busy to pay attention to her.

This situation changed with a minor incident in Sydney, Australia. The executive running our Australian operations was leaving a concert that we promoted in Sydney. As he waited with a crush of people for the parking valet to bring his car, he heard the head valet announce this woman's name and that her limousine was ready. Until that moment our executive had no idea that she was in Sydney or what business she was conducting there. He was particularly intrigued by her use of a limousine (which is not a sanctioned expense).

This was our first signal to scrutinize her activities, and she ultimately left our organization.

If there is a lesson for managers to learn from the varying public profiles of employees, I suppose it is this: By all means, encourage your people to cultivate a profile commensurate with their talents and position, but be on guard for any signs that someone's profile is at odds with his or her standing in the company. They may be spending more time advancing their own personal agenda than yours.

EVERY EMPLOYEE HAS A MENTAL YARDSTICK FOR PERSONAL SUCCESS

I think everyone in business has a mental yardstick for their on-the-job performance, a secret form of measurement that motivates them and tells them how they're doing. For many people, the obvious yardstick is money. For others it may be status or control or being liked by everyone or having the freedom to come and go as they please.

My mental yardstick is time. As faithful readers may have guessed by now, I'm a fanatic about maximizing not only my days and hours but my minutes and seconds. Everything I do is filtered through the clock. Everyday business decisions such as where I travel and who I meet are guided by how much time they require of me and how much reward will result from the investment of that time. If the time investment outweighs the reward, I'll usually say no to an opportunity to which other less time-conscious executives might say yes.

For example, unlike many sales executives, I will not fly on the spur of the moment from New York to Los Angeles solely for a meeting that has a vague chance of ending up in a sale. I know a lot of salespeople who would rush to the airport for such a meeting (and in my younger days I would have, too, because letting any sales lead slip by used to torment me). But in my mind nowadays, the five hours in the air each way represent an entire business day wasted. If I stayed in New York, I could cram a dozen or more productive meetings into those ten hours. So I stay put—and save my trip to Los Angeles for a more propitious date when I can make that meeting and several others as well.

This eye-on-the-clock approach colors everything I do.

The good news here, I humbly submit, is that I probably accomplish a lot more in a normal day than most people do. It is also a good management tool—because when people in our company see me being careful with my time, they tend to become more responsible with their hours, minutes, and seconds, too.

The bad news is that I tend to rush through and treat with a broad brush a lot of subjects that would probably benefit from more of my attention. In meetings where I have a lot of points to cover in a specific amount of time, I'm constantly prodding people to move along, even though I know that digressions are often the most interesting and valuable parts. I also suspect that I sometimes appear abrupt, if not rude, to people who aren't aware of my time-consciousness.

But the larger point I'm trying to make is not what my mental yardstick says about me, but what it should be saying to people who deal with me.

A person who knows that time is my yardstick can get a lot more out of me than someone who doesn't appreciate it. They can use my yardstick to persuade, impress, and control me.

If the head of our office in New Zealand thinks it's worthwhile for me to visit there, he's more likely to get me to make the trip if he crowds my schedule with high-level meetings from 6 A.M. to 6 P.M. than if my schedule is only half full. He's telling me in advance that I won't be wasting my time.

Though our company is too big for me to know every employee by name, I will make the time to meet any employee who writes me a note that says, "I need to talk to you for fifteen minutes at your convenience." That "fifteen minutes" is critical. I would be reluctant to meet with someone who neglected to mention how much time he or she needed. A time-specific request impresses me. An open-ended one scares me.

As a manager, I'm always trying to figure out an employee's mental yardstick, seeking clues in his speech, appearance, and work habits to answer the question: How does this individual measure personal happiness and success?

If I can figure out the unit of measurement, I can usually figure out how to manage them. I haven't run into many employees whose mental yardstick is time, but here are four common yardsticks to look for:

1. MONEY.

Money may be the universal unit of measurement for keeping score in business, but some employees try to conceal their feelings about it. However, an employee's true feelings about money are inevitably revealed at salary review time. That's when a normally agreeable or docile individual can turn into a rapacious dynamo who has itemized the dollar value of every contribution he has made at work during the previous year. There's nothing wrong with this. I actually prefer dealing with these types, because they're so direct. Their effort on the job is in direct proportion to their monetary reward. It's not clouded by "warm and fuzzy" factors like recognition or praise or self-esteem. It's commerce in its simplest form: quid pro quo.

2. STATUS.

Status is a trickier yardstick to manage—because (a) it's not a private matter like money and (b) one employee's obsession with status can have a snowball effect on everyone else in the organization. You can't give one employee a bigger job title or office (two of the more obvious status indicators in the workplace) and not expect his peers to seek a comparable title or office. If status is one employee's yardstick, it soon becomes the yardstick for his peers. As a manager I pay extra attention to the status seekers on the staff, because if they get out of control, the entire organization can get out of control.

3. BEING LIKED BY EVERYONE.

Some people simply want to be liked by everyone. They are helpful, accommodating, and reluctant to make waves. They gauge their success by how well they get along. Again, there's nothing wrong with this. It's nice to work with pleasant people. But as a manager, you might not want these types in positions where hard decisions need to be made. The company might be better off filling those slots with people who don't care if everyone likes them.

4. AUTONOMY.

Some people measure happiness and success by how much they can control their own destiny. They will sacrifice money and status for the sense that they have autonomy at work, that no one is looking over their shoulder, questioning their whereabouts, and judging their every move. As a manager I've found this is the easiest yardstick to accommodate. As long as the employee performs as expected, I leave him or her alone.

THE CHANGE OF COMMAND
TELLS ALL

There are many ways to assess an individual's leadership skills. Can they rally the troops in a crisis? Can they motivate through their oratory skills? Do they lead by fiat or by example? Are they liberal or stingy with praise and recognition? Can they instruct as well as lead?

But perhaps the most revealing sign of a true leader happens when the leader, inevitably, moves on to a new post. You can tell more in that transition period about the kind of loyalty and respect an individual commands than you could in months of watching his or her management routine. Some managers easily display all the superficial leadership skills—the erect bearing, the rousing pep talks, the coolness in a crisis—but if the troops are genuinely relieved when this type of boss moves on, in my mind that doesn't say much about his brand of leadership.

My friend Ben Bidwell, who eventually held top positions at Ford, Hertz, and Chrysler, once told me one of his proudest professional moments was early in his career at Ford Motor Company. Bidwell was in charge of the Ford sales force in Cleveland in the mid-1960s. He did such a good job in Cleveland that, after a couple of years, he was assigned to run the entire mid-Atlantic territory out of Philadelphia. On the day that he left for Philadelphia, his entire team of thirty salespeople accompanied him from Cleveland to Philadelphia. When they arrived, the Cleveland sales force hosted a dinner for the Philadelphia office in honor of Bidwell. They wanted their Philadelphia colleagues to know exactly what kind of boss they were getting. That single moment—when there's a transition of leaders—speaks volumes about Bidwell's leadership skills.

I also think you can tell a lot about leaders by how easy or difficult they make it for their successor during a transition. Rover Rees, a loyal reader of my newspaper column, once wrote to me with a sterling example of how to handle a change of leadership.

Rees was a pilot in the Marine Corps in 1962. It was a tight squadron that felt great personal loyalty to their Commanding Officer. At some point, the C.O. was relieved and reassigned to another command. His successor happened to be an old friend. At the change-of-command ceremony, the departing C.O., who was well aware of the squadron's loyalty to him and realized that the new C.O. would face some resentment, decided to do a favor for his friend. He introduced the new C.O. and told the squadron what a great pilot he was. "In fact," he said, "I'll show you how good he is." The two officers then got into separate planes and staged a dogfight in which the new C.O. was clearly the better man.

As I say, you can learn almost everything you need to know about leaders during a change of command.

• • •
THE McCORMACK RULES

- Clear details, not "vision," are what employees carry with them from day to day.

- The surest sign of a leader is his or her ability to say, "Do it now!" and it gets done.

- A company where the authority figures have the employees' best interests at heart (and the employees know that) will outlive a company where they don't.

- In our eagerness to delegate as much as we can, sometimes we're better off doing things ourselves.

- If status is one employee's yardstick, it soon becomes the yardstick for his peers.

- You can learn almost everything you need to know about leaders during a change of command.

CHAPTER 4

Hiring the Best Talent and Keeping It

YOU CAN'T RENT A HEART

I've always thought that the biggest hiring mistake you can make is not hiring people who are smarter than you are. As advertising guru David Ogilvy once said (I'm paraphrasing), "If you always hire people slightly dumber than you are, you will build a company of dwarfs. If, on the other hand, you always hire people slightly smarter than you are, you will build a company of giants."

I still believe that, but over the years I've come to amend that philosophy slightly: The second-biggest hiring mistake is forgetting what's inside a person's heart.

A lot of us, when we're evaluating job candidates, tend to be so impressed by braininess, by what's inside a person's head, that we seriously undervalue the passion that person brings to an enterprise. You can rent a brain, but you can't rent a heart. The candidate has to throw that in for free.

I didn't fully appreciate this until some years ago when I was one of a half dozen people on the search committee for a new president of a privately held engineering company. We went about the search in what seemed to me like a rigorous, almost scientific manner. We listed our criteria and then judged each candidate against the list. We had firm ideas about the next president's experience, demeanor, salesmanship, organizational skills, financial acumen, public image, and standing within the industry.

After several months we had a short list of four candidates. Three of them were not quite right, but one seemed perfect. He was smart and, we all agreed, appeared "presidential" (whatever that means!). Mr. Perfect got the job.

Within a year he was gone, leveraging his presidency at the company to a similar title at an even bigger enterprise.

Our search committee reassembled and, again, drew up a short list of four candidates. One of the losers from the previous search made this new short list (the two other losers were no longer interested), but based on our criteria he was the least attractive candidate on the list. He was slightly disheveled. He had little sales experience and never cultivated much of an image within the industry. Still, his name kept popping up. He was an engineer and had run a successful operation elsewhere. His father had been the company's lawyer and a long-time member of the board of directors. As a student he had worked summers at the company. Most of all, though, he obviously cared about the company.

After much wringing of hands on our part, he got the nod. In other words, we gave the presidency to the biggest wild card on our list. I'm happy to report that he has turned out to be the best president the company has ever had. The employees love him. As an engineer himself, he really understands how engineers think. And it shows on the bottom line.

I learned a couple of things from this experience.

For one thing, our hiring criteria were wrong. We constructed a menu of things that the new president would have to be able to do. Then we started looking for someone who could match all or most of our list of desirable qualities. It never occurred to us that our list could be wrong.

Most important, it never occurred to us that our priorities were askew, that we ranked the criteria in the wrong order. We were looking for a leader who was smart, experienced, presentable, fiscally responsible, etc.—in that order. In hindsight, the number one attribute we needed was *passion for the enterprise*. If we had ten attributes, ranked from 1 to 10, I suspect that sort of passion would be more important than the other nine combined. Passion is what our first choice lacked and what our second (and successful) choice had in abundance.

As I say, you can rent a person's head but you can't rent a heart.

Whenever I've shared this hiring insight with other executives, few if any of them challenge it. Given the choice between a brainy but ambivalent candidate and an almost-brainy candidate who is totally committed to the organization, they'll always choose the latter.

A magazine editor I know amplified the point. "What many people forget," he said, "is that you don't have to look far and wide for this sort of passion among employees."

115

He told me about the time he had to replace his picture editor. Since quality graphics was such a vital part of the magazine, he was going to take his time and find the best picture editor in the business. But the assistant picture editor wouldn't let him have that luxury. He wanted the job and lobbied very hard for it. The editor thought that, in temperament and experience, the assistant wasn't ready for the top spot. He talked too much. He wasn't a "big respected name" among photographers. And the editor knew he could never rein him in on expenses; he would always overpay for pictures. Despite these personal misgivings, the editor gave the assistant a shot. He named him Acting Picture Editor.

Within a few months the "Acting" was removed from his title. It was clear that he was the best choice all along. He may not have had the credentials, the professional standing, or the polished interpersonal skills the editor thought he needed. But the assistant was obsessed with getting the best photos into the magazine.

That sort of passion can't be bought or manufactured. It outweighs almost any other attribute. Most interesting, though, you can usually find it right under your nose, among the people you already employ.

BUILDING DEPTH IN YOUR EXECUTIVE RANKS

As a manager you always want to do everything in your power to help your people advance upward in the organization. If employees see that you care about their career, they'll work harder for you. It also reflects well on you. If the people under you consistently show greater gains in power, prestige, or compensation than people in other areas of the company, that says something positive about your ability to identify and develop executive talent. Eventually the best people will want to work for you—because you provide the best chance for success.

But helping people advance in the organization begs the question: What is advancement? Is it more money? A fancier title? A bigger office? More perks? A fatter expense account?

It varies among employees. Everyone defines personal success differently. But over the years I've learned that the most obvious form of advancement—namely, the bigger title—is also the most complicated. Sometimes a bigger title can be a curse.

In the standard corporate pyramid, where the job titles range from CEO to Executive Vice President to Senior VP to VP, a lot of companies seem to think that every increase in an executive's authority or responsibility must be accompanied by a commensurate increase in title. An energetic VP running one project is asked to take over a new project as well. Since he's running two projects—twice the budget, twice the people, twice the responsibility—he's given the heftier title of Senior VP. The trouble with this, of course, is what do you do if the new project doesn't pan out or the new Senior VP fails? Suddenly you're stuck with a Senior VP who has the title but not the responsibility.

To me this is putting the cart before the horse. I'd much rather pile the responsibilities on a rising executive and withhold the title until he proves himself. That virtually guarantees the promotion's success. When it is formally announced, it only confirms what everyone knows about the executive.

Fewer people will question his new status—because everyone will know that he earned it.

As a manager, you develop depth in your organization not by giving people better titles but by giving them more work and by carefully choosing the kind of work you give them.

If I give a promising but unheralded executive in our company the job of managing a top-ranked client, that automatically boosts the executive's standing in and out of the company—because of who the client is. When you consciously give someone a high-profile assignment, you're grooming rather than promoting them. But the effect is sometimes greater than a promotion.

Likewise, if we ask one of our television executives to produce a program that is far more elaborate than anything he's ever done, the fact that we chose him is more significant to him and gives him more credibility and prestige with his peers and the outside world than if we gave him a bigger title and no responsibilities.

There are other little things managers can do to groom people before promoting them.

You can praise people for a job well done in a widely distributed memo. That always catches people's attention—and lets them know who the rising stars in the organization are.

You can give people troubleshooting assignments to see how they deal with people in other areas and how they handle problems outside their normal area of expertise.

My personal favorite is including rising stars in certain meetings. It may not seem like much to invite a junior executive to sit in on a senior management meeting, but doing so vests that individual with almost as much status as a promotion. You'd be surprised how that simple act of inclusion affects the people who attended the meeting and, more dramatically, the people who didn't.

P.S.: When it comes time to actually announce an executive promotion, I've learned that it's often better to do it quietly rather than with a lot of fanfare.

Like most bosses, I used to announce promotions in company-wide memos. You know the type: "It is my pleasure to announce that Joe Smith has been named vice president in charge of the Eastern territory. . . ." I did so because that's the way everybody did it, because it boosted the ego and profile of Joe Smith, and because it let everyone know what Joe Smith's new responsibilities were.

Unfortunately, I didn't count on the ripple effect such memos have on all the people who didn't receive a new title or promotion. Instead of functioning as statements of "who does what" in the company, these memos took on an added dimension—as if they were report cards on who's gaining and who's falling behind. I was besieged by executives who wanted the same title as their peer Joe Smith. This invariably led to a new round of title inflation.

For the past five years, I've taken a different approach to promotions. No memos. No big noises. I only tell the executive who's receiving the new title—as if it's our secret. Given the nature of business organizations, it's not a secret for long. News of the promotion filters down through the company quickly and efficiently—to everyone who needs to know. Which is just the way I want it.

HIRE THE ONE WHO BEAT YOU

A few years ago the daughter of a friend moved to New York City to make her mark as an actress. It wasn't long before she found an agent and started going on auditions for theater work, soap operas, and commercials. She struck paydirt with the advertising agencies and casting directors who hire actors for TV commercials. She had ability, of course, but she also had the right look. Within one ten-day span she was "booked" for three national commercials for an auto company, a credit card, and a brand of coffee.

Shortly thereafter, she began getting daily messages on her answering machine from another agent. The message was always the same: "Hi, Dana. I know you're busy. I think it would be worthwhile for you to visit our offices and have a talk. Call me."

She ignored these messages at first, partly out of naiveté (she didn't know who this other agent was), partly out of loyalty (she was very happy with her current agent).

She eventually learned that the agent calling her was a very powerful woman who, indeed, could really help her career. So she returned the call.

"I keep getting these messages that you want to talk with me," she said, "and I'm curious about why, out of all the actors out there, you've chosen me."

The woman replied, "Because our best client has been the runner-up on the last three commercial auditions we gave her. And each time we ask who got the job, they tell us it's you."

That brief exchange speaks volumes about why that agent has such a powerful reputation. She doesn't take defeat lightly or lying down. Nor does she sulk or make excuses about the set-back. She takes action. If someone beats her, she tries to make that person her own.

This "hire the one who beat you" tactic is one of the best ways for an entrepreneur to rapidly improve his or her management ranks. It's also one of the least used and appreciated tactics—perhaps because some entrepreneurs are uncomfortable with the idea of raiding the competition. You have to be daring and a touch ruthless to attempt it; you have to feel some disdain for your competitors to enjoy it; and you need fortitude and savvy when they turn the tables and try to raid you.

However, the advantages of hiring the one who beat you are considerable. You not only improve your business but you damage your rival's business. Your gain is their loss.

Being aware of the benefits of this tactic, you should also be aware of how you can become its victim. Some people go to Machiavellian extremes when they hire away the competition—and their reasons for doing so are rarely what they seem. Consider the following story, which a friend told me over lunch, as a cautionary example.

Apparently a wealthy European industrialist was trying to merge two companies that he controlled. At some point he realized that the merger would never work because the management styles of the two companies were too far apart. Company A was a lean, cost-conscious operation with a small headquarters staff and spartan offices. Company B went overboard the other way; it was your basic bloated and cancerous hierarchy, with lavish offices, superfluous layers of managers, out-of-control costs, and a CEO who used corporate resources to advance himself within the community.

The industrialist feared that, in a merger, the cancerous style of Company B (which he detested) would spread to Company A and give it cancer, too. So he took evasive action.

He identified the worst executive at Company B—that is, the most egregious offender of corporate excess—and orchestrated a scenario where he was forced to resign. Then the industrialist hired him as a consultant, on the theory that this executive knew where all the skeletons were buried at Company B and was so angry at his former employers for forcing him out that he would be eager to reveal those skeletons.

It was a brilliant move. With the angry consultant by his side showing him the way, the industrialist surgically removed all the remaining cancerous elements at Company B, including the CEO. After that it was relatively easy to install Company A's management at the top of the newly merged organization—and the merger has worked out.

WHEN YOU CAN'T AFFORD THE BEST

Hiring people smarter than you are is nice advice if you can afford it. But what do you do when you're a startup company, or when you're not the market leader, or when your competitors have a pay scale that dramatically outscales yours? What do you do when you can't afford the best?

Writing a big check is not the only way to hire the best people. In fact, offering the most money may be the worst way to hire great people. If money is your only selling point, all you're doing is assembling a cast of talented mercenaries. They may be professionals who do an excellent job, but what's stopping them from jumping ship when a better offer comes along? Here are four less costly strategies for luring talent.

1. THE FUN FACTOR.

If you ask talented people why they left a seemingly good job for another, they'll often tell you, "The old job wasn't fun anymore." If there's one compelling reason that good people leave or stay at a job, it boils down to this: *Talented people want to get paid for doing a job they would be willing to do for free.* (That's the reasoning behind the U.S. Army's memorable recruiting slogan: "It's not a job. It's an adventure.")

Of course, all of us have our own definition of "fun on the job."

To an engineer it might be the chance to work with cutting-edge technology.

To a computer wizard it might be the chance to work with people as smart as he thinks he is.

To a veteran manager it might be the challenge of a hopeless turnaround situation.

To a middle manager with a young family it might mean a relocation to a place with a more attractive lifestyle.

To a college graduate it might be working with a lot of like-minded young people.

To a powerful CEO it might be more power. (That's why very successful people in the private sector will accept an important position in government at a fraction of the salary; power is a more potent lure than money, especially to people who already have enough money.)

If you know what a talented prospect regards as fun on the job (hint: ask him or her) and can satisfy that desire at your company, you can afford almost anybody.

2. PURSUE RELENTLESSLY.

A lot of managers forget that luring good people to their side is in part a seduction process—which takes time and relentless wooing. I'm not sure if these managers are too proud to go back to a prospect after the first rejection or they don't have the time. But they all seem to forget that steady pursuit may be a nuisance to some people but it is inherently flattering to everyone.

Think about how you would feel if someone, out of the blue, asked you to come work for them. Think about how you would feel if they came back a second, third, or fourth time after you said no. Unless they were absolutely obnoxious about it, in which case you should send them packing, the more times they contact you the better the chance that they'll win you over. Eventually the pursuer will come up with an argument that turns his quarry around.

That's the real secret behind relentless pursuit. If a talented prospect knows you can't afford him but is still listening to your overtures, there's a part of him that secretly wants to be wooed. He's probably waiting for you to convince him.

3. RESCUE THE SUFFERING.

Talented people don't always make the right career choices. Some of them are languishing in the wrong job. Some are stuck at an organization that, for whatever reason, may be on the way down. If you keep an eye on your field, you should know which companies are thriving and which are not, and you should also have an idea which of the quality people at those companies are happy and which are not.

If you can offer a rescue line to people on a sinking ship, you will rarely have to pay a premium price for their talents. They will not only jump to your side, they will do so with gratitude.

4. RECRUIT THE YOUNG.

I have learned that the easiest way to get good people at bargain rates is to recruit them straight out of college. A lot of managers neglect this route, contending that they want "someone with experience." But I've always been skeptical about the value of experience. It not only costs you a considerable amount more to get it, but who can say that experience is right for your organization?

In the 1960s and 1970s, we built our company by hiring a lot of smart M.B.A.'s from the best schools. Part of this was practicality (we could afford them). But we also knew that "experience" was meaningless in our business. Sports marketing was so unique that there weren't many, if any, people with legitimate expertise. Our company was writing the rules as we went along. So we hired the best young people we could find, with no experience, and taught them how we wanted things done.

I recommend this strategy to anyone building a company from the ground up.

THE DANGER OF HIRING SOMEONE ELSE'S SUPERSTAR

A few years ago a friend of mine, the owner of a thriving design group, made what he thought was a masterstroke of hiring. He hired the creative director of the advertising agency that was handling his company's account to join his firm.

This ad executive was an industry superstar and the move cost my friend dearly. He gave his new superstar a huge salary and equity in the company if he stayed two years. He provided him with his own car and carte blanche on expenses. The move puzzled a lot of people in the industry. Within ten months, though, the superstar quit to form his own design company. In hindsight, it appears that the superstar was using my friend to subsidize his entry into the design business.

In a way, the outcome was a foregone conclusion. The dangers of hiring someone else's superstar are great—and it's the rare situation that has a happy ending.

The biggest problem I have with hiring someone else's superstar is that it promotes managerial laziness.

In my mind, it's a much smarter investment to hire three $50,000 executives than one $150,000 executive. Making the investment pay off takes a little work, of course. You have to spend a lot of time training the $50,000 executives. But if you train them well, you stand a good chance of having one or more superstars in your company one day.

Another problem: A superstar in one environment is not necessarily going to be a superstar in yours.

We've made this mistake more than once. When Arnold Palmer was starting his first auto dealership, he brought in the general manager of a Big Three auto division to run it, figuring that this fellow knew the industry. Unfortunately, he knew it as a manufacturer, not a dealer. He knew how to manage engineers, designers, factory foremen. He was accustomed to having a huge support staff and dealing with ten-figure budgets. But he knew very little about a small business and dealing face-to-face with the buying public. He was a superstar, yes. But not for us.

Then there is also the fuzzy criteria people use to identify superstars. Quite often we equate a big salary and fancy title with superstardom. If the senior vice president of sales at a company is earning, say, $300,000 a year, he must be a great salesman. Yet in truth, he may have arrived at that position and salary level through a wide variety of circumstances, none of which you know. Perhaps the company gave him the title because it made him happy or in lieu of more money. Or maybe the company hired him a few years earlier at a high salary because someone else was paying him too much. Now he's getting tiny annual raises, but he's still overpaid.

The upshot of all this is that the superstar arrives at the new company more as a problem than a solution. His new colleagues may resent his big salary and big title. The boss who hired him probably expects him to perform miracles immediately. Is it any wonder that someone else's superstar fizzles more often than he shines?

PAY ATTENTION TO ATTENTION SPANS

As managers we all know the standard criteria for assessing the value of our employees, *e.g.*, intelligence, initiative, ambition, loyalty, decisiveness, adaptability. Let me introduce one more criterion, equally important, which, for lack of a better term, I call "attention span."

I think every employee can be judged by his or her attention span on the job. I use the phrase not in the narrow sense of how many minutes someone can stay focused on a particular task but in the much broader sense of how many days or weeks or years someone can stay interested in their job.

For example, at our company we have a wide range of attention spans.

We have people in our legal, financial, and accounting departments who have been doing essentially the same job for two or three decades. In terms of attention span, they are long-distance runners. They are fulfilled and stimulated by the subtle differences in contracts or tax problems or spreadsheets. There's nothing wrong with this. On the contrary, these departments would be a mess if we didn't hire people with this admirable sort of staying power.

Then there are the middle-distance runners, the employees who can stay focused on a job for four to six years and then feel the need for a change. They switch to another division, change companies, or in some cases totally reinvent themselves in a new profession in a new locale. In my experience, people in this category tend to have good people skills, which may explain why they're comfortable moving around so often. If you can deal with people, you can do well in many jobs. (You can identify these types by looking at their résumé and noting how they change jobs every few years.)

We also have people who, in terms of attention span, can only be characterized as sprinters. They prefer short-term assignments with clearly defined start and stop dates. They get bored or frustrated when they cannot see the light at the end of the tunnel. These are the kinds of people who thrive in the event implementation side of our business. They can get fired up working for three months on a volleyball event in Los Angeles. When that event ends, they can put it behind them and get equally enthusiastic about a tennis tournament in Houston or a motor race in Detroit. You could argue that the main attraction of the job to them is not the chance to work on a sports event but rather the fact that the job regularly mutates into something else. They like the steady change of scenery. Again, there's nothing wrong with being a sprinter. Our company would be lost without them.

The crucial test for a manager, of course, is to make sure that an employee's attention span matches up with the job he or she is doing. You don't want "sprinters" in your accounting department because they'll be gone before they've learned your system. Nor do you want your "long-distance runners" working on a three-week event because it will be over before they catch their stride.

The management lesson here is simple to understand: If an organization is suffering from high employee turnover, perhaps the people who are involved in hiring decisions should start paying attention to employee attention spans.

WHAT CREATIVE PEOPLE
REALLY WANT

I once had to referee a dispute between a capable manager and one of his equally able subordinates. The two of them didn't see eye-to-eye on anything. After talking to each of them, I saw why.

The subordinate was a creative fellow who had developed several clever concepts for us. As is sometimes (not always) the case with creative people, he was undisciplined if not unruly. He didn't keep predictable hours. He didn't always tell his boss or his colleagues what he was working on or where he was. He truly believed his so-called creativity gave him a license to flout an organization's rules and common courtesies. As long as he regularly produced good ideas, he could afford to act the part of a corporate free spirit.

Predictably, this drove his boss nuts. The subordinate was uncontrollable in precisely those areas that a good manager needs to control. All managers (even those who keep very loose reins on their staff) need to know what their people are working on, where they are when they're not in the office, what they have achieved lately, and what projects have fallen by the wayside. If nothing else, managers need to know this so they can keep their bosses informed.

I told the subordinate that he had to be a little more communicative about his activities. I told the manager to expect a little less from his unruly charge. But this was a classic standoff between a rogue employee and a boss who wouldn't give special treatment to someone who considered himself special.

In the end I settled the standoff in blunt fashion: I transferred the subordinate to a more tolerant manager. The alternative would have been to retrain the manager in the fine art of handling creative people. If I had to do it over again, though, I would have retrained the manager in the fine art of handling creatives. Here's where I would start.

1. Revere creativity.

If new ideas are the lifeblood of any thriving organization (and, trust me, they are), managers must learn to revere, not merely tolerate, the people who come up with those ideas. Sounds obvious, doesn't it? But it's incredible how often people forget this. I've seen lots of organizations where managers and salespeople actually resent their creative people.

This resentment manifests itself in many ways. I've seen sales executives obsessed with chipping away at the research and development budget so they can spend it on sales and marketing. I've seen managers deride, then try to control, the unstructured work habits of creative people, as if creativity can be confined to the hours between 9 A.M. and 5 P.M. I've heard salespeople scoff at the "ivory tower" existence of the people who devote all their waking hours to dreaming up new products or services. Closing deals and creating revenue, they boast, is where "the rubber meets the road."

None of this reveals a reverence for creativity. Before you can manage creative people, you must learn to appreciate them.

2. Acknowledge creativity.

More than anything, creative people (a) want credit for their ideas and (b) loathe managers who try to steal credit for their ideas. Whenever you have an impulse to praise someone for a brilliant idea, act on it. If you have a simultaneous impulse to share in that glory (deserved or otherwise), stifle it.

3. Ideas or revenue? You decide.

In many companies there's a Chinese wall separating the creative people from the people who are expected to generate revenue from that creativity. At a magazine, for example, the editorial staff produces the words and pictures; the sales force sells the advertising. The best magazines try to make a virtue of this "church and state" division. They want to foster the impression that the editorial and business sides never talk, that the editor-in-chief is unmoved by outside interference and never considers advertising when assigning stories.

It's an interesting fantasy, but the truth is more interesting. I've known business-savvy editors who are keenly interested in ad pages and can stand up in front of an audience of potential advertisers and sell the magazine as well as, if not better than, their colleagues on the business side.

In my mind, the distinction between creatives coming up with the ideas and non-creatives generating revenue is wholly artificial and serves no one well. It applies to some people, but not to everyone. I'm sure there are brilliant software designers at Microsoft or Lotus who would be perfectly happy if they never had to wear a jacket and tie and attend a business meeting. Likewise, I'm sure there are equally brilliant designers who would not only love to tell the sales force how to sell their program but actually go out on the road and do it.

At our company there's virtually no distinction between generating ideas and generating revenue. The people who come up with a good idea are generally expected to make money out of it, too. They may have to enlist some help from colleagues to sell the concept internally and externally, but if the idea's creator can't drive the project, who can?

My point is that creative people don't fit a tidy stereotype. Some want to be left alone in their ivory tower. Some want to break out. Treat each person accordingly.

4. COMPENSATE CREATIVELY.

Money isn't always the primary driving force behind the long hours that creative people put in at work. Sometimes money takes a back seat to a desire for autonomy or recognition or simply an environment where people can do their best work.

At our company, some of my easiest salary negotiations have been with talented people who gladly sacrificed their annual raise for an extra week's vacation or less paperwork and administrative duties. More free time and more freedom from bureaucracy was infinitely more important to them than money.

Most managers never think of including these features in the corporate compensation package, but with creative people, they should.

IT'S THE COVER LETTER, NOT THE RÉSUMÉ, THAT COUNTS

I'm always a little amazed by the extremes that people take in preparing their résumé. They spend hours, perhaps days, working and reworking every line describing their professional experience. Then they show the résumé to friends, inviting suggestions which inevitably induce another round of corrections. Then they choose a typeface that "expresses" their personality. Some people even spend hours deciding on the color, weight, and texture of the paper the résumé is printed on.

Don't get me wrong. I'm not knocking people who take the time to produce a smart résumé that accentuates their virtues. But all that effort seems a little misguided. I think people greatly overestimate the scrutiny their résumés receive out in the marketplace. Perhaps they think that their future employer can read between the lines of their résumé and somehow plumb the essence of their soul or find clues that prove their unworthiness as a candidate.

The real story is much more mundane.

For most people at most companies, reviewing résumés is a straightforward process that takes seconds rather than minutes or hours. They match the candidate's experience with the job. If they are looking for a sales manager, they toss out any résumé that doesn't contain sales experience. In that context, there really are no mysteries, no hidden clues in a résumé.

I know I don't spend too much time trying to read between the lines of a résumé. If I have questions, I can get a straight answer in our interview.

I suppose if I were more alert or devoted more time to the matter I could detect some clues in a résumé. After all, some red flags flap in front of your face. But they may also lead to flawed conclusions. If a candidate has changed jobs every ten months for the last four years, that may indicate a jumpiness and instability you might not want at your company. But then again, the candidate may have a valid reason for each move, anything from layoffs to spouse relocation. You'll never know unless you meet the candidate face-to-face. If you misread that red flag, you may miss out on a great employee.

In my experience, the cover letter that accompanies the résumé is a far more revealing document and a better indicator of a candidate's worthiness. Résumés, by definition, are generic. They adhere to a rigid format and, after so much massaging and polishing, they totally lack any personality. They could belong to anyone.

Cover letters, on the other hand, require some ingenuity. That's where the standout candidates actually stand out.

A well-written cover letter tells me something about the candidate's ability to articulate his or her thoughts. (A cover letter written in the dry, artificial tones of memospeak tells me something too, although it's hardly positive.)

A cover letter that misspells my name tells me something about the candidate's precision, or lack thereof.

A cover letter that contains a clever idea is a sign of bold thinking—and not the sort of thing normally gleaned from a résumé.

Almost anything is a clue. I once received an impressive résumé, but what tipped the scales for the candidate was her cover letter and the fact that she took the time to type in the correct French accents on the word "résumé." A small sign, perhaps, but just the sort of perfectionism that was needed in one of our divisions. I passed her name on to an executive in need of an assistant. Not surprisingly, she was as impressive in person as in writing—and got the job.

Don't Forget to Sell Your Newest Hire

Whenever managers hire or promote someone to a new position, they are faced with a critical choice in how they present that new person within the company. They can (a) aggressively sell the new person's talents and potential or (b) they can take the passive route, letting the new person prove himself on his own. Since circumstances vary with each new hire or promotion, I suppose a valid case could be made for either approach. But my personal preference is to aggressively sell the new person to his peers.

I really wasn't aware that a choice existed until a friend pointed out that I always did this. I had just given a young but worthy executive a major bump up in responsibilities at our company and, apparently, was singing his praises every chance I got.

My friend noticed the change of tune and called me on it. "You know, Mark," he said, "this fellow has been working for you for nine years, but I've never heard you even mention his name until he got this new promotion."

I suppose there's a logical explanation for this. With his new promotion, this executive and I had more contact with each other and, consequently, I had more opportunities to observe him in action. But on reflection I think I was also selling his promotion. By advertising my elevated opinion of him, I could elevate other people's opinion of him as well. This, in turn, would make him more effective and would increase the chances that the promotion would be a success.

It's a self-fulfilling approach, which makes it all the more puzzling why so many managers ignore it. Rather than assist their newest hire or promotion, they (consciously or otherwise) resist it. This resistance manifests itself in many subtle ways.

For example, we have one senior executive in our company who insists on personally reporting all his division's activities himself. If I call him up to ask "What's new?" he'll tell me about five ongoing deals on three continents. I'm sure he realizes that I know he cannot physically manage all those transactions alone. Yet he'll never mention his associates who are doing all the work. The implication is that he is doing all those deals himself. I suppose he thinks that crediting his subordinates will somehow diminish him in my eyes. Actually, it would make him seem bigger.

The interesting thing about selling a new employee is how easy it is to do, at no expense to your ego, dignity, or reputation if you follow these five simple steps:

1. Don't forget the ringing endorsement. This is the most rudimentary advice, yet people still forget it. Instead of citing all the positive reasons why they hired or promoted the new person in the first place ("He turned around XYZ Company's sales force in a year" or "Everybody told me he's the best MIS guy on the East Coast"), they shrug off his arrival as a non-event ("I hope he works out" or "It may take him some time to learn our ways . . ."). The latter is hardly a ringing endorsement. If I were the newly hired or promoted person, I'd prefer my boss didn't comment on me at all.

2. Urge people to get to know the new person. When a new hire or promotion doesn't work out, it's often because

people in the company didn't appreciate the significance
of his arrival or what he was capable of. I am constantly ca-
joling our executives to meet new people in our company.
If I know that Joe Jones is working in an area that the new
person, Tom Smith, is familiar with, I will write Joe Jones
to say, "Tom Smith knows more about this area than anyone in our company. Before you proceed any further, you
should spend some time going over this with him. . . ." That
kind of memo sells the new person more effectively than
any compliment.

3. Give him high-visibility assignments. As a manager you
can't always wait for your new person to find his special
niche within the company. You sometimes have to create the niche by giving him high-profile assignments—
e.g., dealing with a major customer, heading up a crucial
project, chairing a task force. The more serious the assignment, the more seriously your new person will be
taken.

4. Bring him to meetings. Quite often, the simple inclusion
of the new person in meetings elevates his status and
credibility. I will often include people in meetings even
though their presence is not absolutely necessary. Doing
so not only lets me introduce them to a totally new set of
characters and contacts, but if, at some point in the meeting, I defer to them and let them demonstrate their expertise, I have enhanced their standing with everyone in
the room.

5. Don't be a roadblock. Like the executive I mentioned above,
a lot of managers are reluctant (or afraid) to expose their

subordinates to the higher ranks of the company. They reserve that privilege for themselves. Of course, the opposite approach is the smarter move. It's one thing to be known as a thoroughbred executive yourself. It's even better to be known as someone who breeds and attracts other thoroughbreds, too.

GIVE PEOPLE TIME TO PROVE THEMSELVES

A good friend once made an interesting observation about our company. He said, "Unless they are total jerks, the only way people can get fired from your company, Mark, is either theft or disloyalty."

That statement is probably closer to the truth than I might care to admit. Given the choice, I think most companies would rather keep people than lose them.

It's not as if people are automatically guaranteed jobs for life once they get a foothold inside our company. I think I'm as performance-driven as the next manager. I'm always looking for new people to prove themselves and weighing their value to the company against the cost of keeping them.

In an ideal world, this should be relatively easy to do. You simply have to be definitive rather than vague about what you expect from a new hire. If we hire a salesperson for the Los Angeles office, it's good business practice to say we expect the new salesperson to bring in x dollars of business by a specific date. Sales quotas and target dates are a cold, objective standard that everyone can agree on. They establish definitively how long you give people to prove themselves.

In the real world, though, many managers are incapable of sticking to the cold, hard facts. They let vague, subjective criteria creep into the equation and cloud their judgment. With all these warm and fuzzy feelings to contend with, it's no wonder a lot of managers (myself included) seem to be creating tenure systems at their companies. Here are four considerations that complicate any answer to the question, "How long do you give people to prove themselves?"

1. When do they hit the ground running?

If you bring in a salesperson at x salary and he's expected to bring in 4x in revenue, is six months unreasonably short? Is a year reasonable? Then when the year is up, do you extend it until one of the salesperson's pending deals comes through?

A few years back we hired an executive who was presented to me as an expert in his particular field, the sort of salesperson who justified his generous compensation because it would take no time to bring him up to speed. He would hit the ground running on Day One.

It didn't work out that way. He was bright and pleasant. Everyone liked him. And he was extremely impressive at meetings, particularly with clients to whom he could talk eloquently on any subject. But he couldn't sell.

Unfortunately, you can't pay people just to be impressive at meetings. Ultimately they have to deliver. But this fellow had enough positives in his favor that we gave him the benefit of the doubt for several years. Except for his inability to bring in revenue, he was a great executive! Eventually he left of his own volition. Had it not been for his voluntary departure, it's quite likely that he would still be with us, all because he was a nice guy who could shine in meetings.

2. ONE BIG HIT.

"The secret in show business," a Hollywood agent once told me, "is one big killing. You can ride that solitary hit for decades." That's certainly true in sports. A middling golfer who happened to win once at Augusta will forever be known as a "former Masters champion." A Frenchman who wins the French Open will be a national hero for life. So will a Briton or Australian whose only major tennis title happens to be Wimbledon. Likewise in team sports, where some American baseball players have been given a lifetime annuity of fame (and some fortune) because they hit a late-inning home run in the World Series.

It's the same in business. It doesn't take much for an employee to become a permanent fixture at a company. All he has to do is bring in one big account early on and he's established his credibility. He can ride the crest of that wave for a long time. That one big hit can cover up a host of sins and cloud a boss's judgment about someone's true worth.

3. BLINDED BY COSMETICS.

We would all like to think we're above judging people by superficial criteria. But the truth is that we can't avoid being

141

persauded or impressed by cosmetics. Sometimes we're forced to accept cosmetics as a key criterion.

In the early days of our company we hired a seasoned advertising executive in our corporate marketing group. He wasn't a world-beater at bringing in new business. But he had a lot of cosmetic pluses going for him. He looked the part, behaved impeccably, and could speak the peculiar patois of advertising and marketing executives. Most important, he was old. Being a young company at the time, we needed that maturity to counter the impression that we were just a bunch of young college grads—which is exactly what we were when we started.

This man's maturity, not his productivity, kept him on the payroll.

4. RELATIVES GET A FREE RIDE.

Relatives probably get more time than anyone to prove themselves. If affability, maturity, or sheer good looks keep some people employed longer than they deserve, then being related to a senior executive or to an important customer is the ultimate free ride. I know in our company it has sometimes taken years to gently remove an employee who was related to an important customer.

The truth is that you're better off not hiring a relative of a customer or client—despite all the goodwill generated by doing so—because you can't fire a relative. (That's one reason so many high-performance companies, such as law firms or investment groups, have anti-nepotism rules. Injecting relatives destroys the clearly meritocratic structure of the organization.)

5. Big deals then excuse no deals now.

An employee's track record is another factor that can blind a manager's assessment of that employee's current performance. Ideally, a manager starts out with certain performance goals for an employee. But those goals get altered by the employee's length of employment. That's why, at some point, people do achieve a sort of tenure at our company.

It's only human nature for us to ease up a little with people who have been working beside us for some time. It may not be rational, but I tend to judge young, unproven people more severely than I judge people who have proven themselves over a long period of time. In a world of "What have you done for me lately?" criteria, there will always be loyal, hardworking people to whom that question doesn't really apply.

These five factors hardly exhaust the many ways a manager's assessment of people's performance can get skewed. But appreciating them is a good first step to avoid building a company where all employees—good or bad—think they have a job for life.

In Search of the Turnaround Hero

The head of a multinational corporation I know was looking for a top-level executive to turn around an important but faltering part of the company. He had gone through the usual motions of finding the right person. He asked two of his favorite subordinates if they were interested in the job, but they were happy where they were. He hired an executive recruiter to work up a short list of candidates. But after six months he was still not close to a decision.

"There just aren't that many people out there with the credentials to handle a turnaround," he said.

I'm sure he was right, but I was puzzled that he thought he could find one at all. Top-level executives don't go around billing themselves as "turnaround artists." They don't hang signs on their door saying, "Senior VP, Turnarounds." First and foremost, they are managers. When thrust into a do-or-die situation, a few of them turn out to have the skills and temperament to revive an organization. But it's hard to detect these qualities until people are actually in the middle of a turnaround situation.

The multinational's chief should have known this. There's no magic mold in business schools or in other organizations that spits out turnaround artists. The best he could hope to find was an executive who had some of the following qualities:

1. Knows when not to be contrary.

To turn around any organization, the new boss certainly has to be willing to challenge the status quo. He has to cultivate a healthy disrespect for "the way we do things around here." That's obvious. If top management had wanted a caretaker, they could have filled the slot with anyone. But to turn things around, the new boss must also know when not to be a contrarian.

A lot of new bosses go into these situations with an everything-you-know-is-wrong attitude. That's understandable. If the people in the company knew what they were doing, they wouldn't be so deep in the hole. But the fact that mistakes were made doesn't necessarily mean that the employees only make mistakes. If a new boss is smart, he doesn't trash everything the people under him did before he arrived. He highlights some of the good they achieved. He knows when to shake things up and when to leave well enough alone.

2. CAN GAIN INSTANT RESPECT.

Turnaround bosses need to win their organization's respect quickly. They don't have time to romance the staff. If they're shrewd, they can do this in a matter of days or weeks.

The easiest way to win respect is to know more than your people do. But circumstances don't always work in your favor.

I once knew a packaged-goods executive who took over a high-tech firm that desperately needed his marketing skills. This fellow realized that, given his background, he would always be at a technical disadvantage with his employees. He would never know as much about the company's sophisticated products as his techies and engineers knew.

So he decided to learn as much as he could about the people. Most new bosses do this during their first days on the job. They call their staffers into their office and interview them. "Tell me a little bit about yourself," they say. This is supposed to create a bond between new boss and staff.

But this fellow had a better plan. He learned everything he could about his staff—from reviewing personnel files and talking to other employees—before his first day on the job.

When he took over, he quickly made sure his subordinates knew that he had done his homework on them. It's hard not to respect someone like that.

3. CAN IDENTIFY THE NUMBER ONE PRIORITY.

In any turnaround, there are so many problems that you don't know which one to tackle first.

A turnaround artist lists his goals—for example, improve administrative practices, cut costs, increase working capital, develop new products, and calm down angry customers—and then has the courage and resolve to pick one as his top priority.

He knows that solving five problems at once is impossible. But concentrating on one top-priority problem gives people a sense of mission. It's also achievable. When they get the problem under control, they have a sense of accomplishment that propels them to the next priority.

4. NOT NECESSARILY AN OUTSIDER.

It's fashionable to go outside the company when you need to stir things up in faltering areas of the organization. But I'm not sure that's always the best policy. I've watched several of my friends follow fairly conventional career paths up the corporate ladder. But when they finally reached a certain level of autonomy, either as a division chief or CEO of a company, they surprised me by how radical and innovative they could be in their new job. In some cases, they not only turned around their company, but they turned their industry upside down.

146

I may have been surprised, but the person who promoted them obviously wasn't. Someone above them in the company was paying attention to them and saw a maverick quality that could shake things up when the time came.

Before you go outside your company to turn things around, take a closer look at your people inside. You may find a hero much closer to home.

• • •
THE McCORMACK RULES

- The biggest hiring mistake is not hiring people smarter than you are.

- The second biggest hiring mistake is forgetting what's inside a person's heart.

- You can rent a brain, but you can't rent a heart. The candidate has to throw that in for free.

- "Hire the one who beat you" and you will immediately improve your management ranks.

- The easiest way to get good people at bargain rates is to recruit them straight out of college.

- The dangers of hiring someone else's superstar are great—and it's the rare situation that has a happy ending.

- A superstar in one environment is not necessarily going to be a superstar in yours.

- All managers (even those who keep very loose reins on their staff) need to know what their people are working on, where they are when they're not in the office, what they have achieved lately, and what projects have fallen by the wayside.

- Whenever you have an impulse to praise someone for a brilliant idea, act on it. If you have a simultaneous impulse to share in that glory (deserved or otherwise), stifle it.

- The more serious the assignment you give a new hire, the more seriously that person will be taken.

- It's one thing to be known as a thoroughbred executive yourself. It's even better to be known as someone who breeds and attracts other thoroughbreds.

- The easiest way to win respect is to know more than your people do.

- Before you go outside your company to turn things around, take a closer look at your people inside. You may find a turnaround hero much closer to home.

CHAPTER 5

Making Smarter Decisions

KEEPING THE DUMB MISTAKES TO A MINIMUM

Ken Iverson, the much-admired chairman of Nucor Steel Corp., is frequently quoted on the subject of why good managers make bad decisions. "The best manager in the world, a guy with a Harvard M.B.A.," says Iverson, "might make bad decisions around 40 percent of the time. And a rotten manager might make bad decisions 60 percent of the time."

Iverson's point is that there's only about a 20 percent difference between a good manager and a rotten one.

But that hasn't stopped him from encouraging aggressive decision making. "As a manager," he says, "you have to make decisions. If you don't make decisions, you are going nowhere and doing nothing. But if you make decisions you will make bad decisions. You have to have a strange and monstrous ego to think that you never make bad decisions."

I wholeheartedly agree with Iverson. But I think 40 percent bad decisions is slightly too tolerant for good managers. I think you can still be an aggressive decision maker and reduce your bad decisions to 25 percent. The key is knowing what kind of decisions are most likely to end up as bad ones—and being more cautious and less aggressive in dealing with those categories. Here are four categories where managers tend to be particularly error-prone.

1. WHEN YOU'RE HIRING.

There are two things to remember about hiring decisions.

First, they are deceptively simple to make but sometimes impossible to recover from. When you hire someone, you are inviting them into your "house" and entrusting them with your resources and reputation. The people you hire can make or break you. It can take you years to realize you've made a mistake—and nearly as long to correct it.

Second, hiring decisions seem to bring out the worst insecurities in people. A top executive hires toadies and then wonders why they have no initiative. A small-business owner deliberately hires people who are "good," but not so good that they'll steal clients and go out on their own. A devoted secretary finds a substandard replacement so she will be fondly remembered and/or sorely missed.

For these two reasons alone you should be more thoughtful and perhaps less rambunctious in the kind of people you invite into your workplace. Good managers who treat hiring decisions casually will soon be rotten managers.

2. WHEN ONE FACT IS MISSING.

You can't delay decisions simply because you don't have all the facts. Sometimes you have to base your decisions on intuition—and take the good with the bad. But I worry when someone tells me they have thoroughly researched a decision. There's always one fact missing, usually in an area beyond their established expertise, that invariably proves them wrong.

Years ago I came to the conclusion that the next growth area in golf would be South America. So we decided to set up a series of golf tournaments in Peru, Venezuela, and Brazil. We knew the economics of a golf event in the U.S., in Europe, in Japan, and in Australia as well as anyone.

We determined that we would need $50,000 in prize money to attract a quality field (this was the early 1960s) and $50,000 more to implement each tournament. We knew that sponsorship and ticket sales would generate $125,000 in revenue, thus resulting in a $25,000 profit per event for us. It seemed like a good idea at the time.

However, we missed one fact: the incredible volatility of national currencies and inflation rates in South America. It was unlike anything we had seen in other parts of the world. By the time the first event took place and inflation had taken its toll, our budget was a joke. Instead of making $25,000, we lost $40,000.

We were experts at golf, not international finance. That fact sent us limping home.

3. WHEN THERE IS NO VOID TO FILL.

South American golf is a good example of how we decide to go into new areas. We look for a void where there's little or no competition and fill it.

Some of our worst decisions have occurred when we strayed from this philosophy, when we ventured into an area that was already crowded with strong competitors.

There was a time in our company when our television executives felt frustrated at the lack of huge numbers in sports television. They thought the big money was in motion pictures—and they somehow persuaded me to back their adventure in Hollywood. Of course, motion pictures is precisely the kind of area that doesn't qualify as a void. There was too much competition. We got eaten alive.

I'm often asked why our company isn't heavily involved in the pop music business and in representing rock stars. The answer is simple: There are too many strong competitors ahead of us. There is no void to fill.

That basic rationale, at least in the area of new ventures, has helped me lower my bad decisions to well below 25 percent. If there is no void to fill, I don't rush in.

4. WHEN THE DRIVING FORCE IS EGO.

There's a difference between having an ego and having an ego problem. A healthy ego gives you the confidence to make bold decisions. An ego problem seduces you into making increasingly bolder decisions—to top your competitors or to top yourself. Eventually your bold decisions become bad ones.

I see this all the time in the sports business, where ego often gets in the way of rational thought.

The most egregious example is the wealthy entrepreneur who decides to buy a sports team. If this otherwise-smart executive treated the purchase of an NFL or Major League Baseball franchise like any other business decision, he would probably walk away. The price of a franchise is at an all-time high. Some second-tier markets are simply not large enough to be profitable. Labor costs (*i.e.*, players' salaries) are out of control. Television audiences, fragmented by cable and satellite TV, are declining. Broadcast rights fees from the networks may shrink in the near future. It's hard to see where the growth potential is. Keeping the money in the bank might be a better investment.

Yet successful businesspeople continue to bid and buy teams. Their ego whispers to them that they deserve this expensive toy. Their ego tells them that they can turn the franchise around. After all, they've been successful before. More often than not, their ego is wrong. The most successful sports franchises (*e.g.*, the Los Angeles Dodgers, Chicago Bears, and New York Giants) tend to be owned by families who've been around a long time. They are run by disciplined managers who can check their ego at the door. They treat the team as a business, not as a toy.

THE PARADOX OF GOOD NEWS

There's a good news/bad news aspect to every fact and number in business. The paradox of good news is that it often blinds us to the bad news.

For example, let's say you are test marketing a new shampoo. Test results from focus groups indicate that 58 percent of consumers love the product. Now, to a lot of people that's an encouraging number. After all, more than half of the respondents said they would buy the shampoo.

The flip side of that number, of course, is that forty-two percent, or nearly half, of the respondents said they don't love the product. That's a problem that many people don't like to dwell on—although they should. They prefer to bask in the warm glow of that 58 percent positive response when, in fact, they might be better off improving a shampoo that forty-two percent of consumers don't like.

That's the dangerous paradox of good news. It seduces you into self-satisfaction and complacency. I see the paradox cropping up in so many ways.

On a personal level, it often has a stultifying effect on an individual's drive and ambition. I've seen this repeatedly in professional sports, among some of the most driven, ambitious, and disciplined individuals I know. A talented tennis player works hard to the point where she is ranked #7 in the world. She rarely loses to anyone ranked below her but almost never beats the players in the top six slots. She can deal with that #7 ranking in two ways: She can revel in the fact that she is #7 and better than hundreds of her peers. It is, after all, an admirable achievement. Or she can turn her attention to the six players above her. She can analyze her game and investigate how (or even if) she can beat her higher-ranked opponents.

I've seen the same behavior in executives when they achieve a certain income level or title at their company. A strange complacency settles in. They find comfort in the good news that they have hit their salary or status goals. They don't look at the flip side of that good news, namely, that if they worked even harder they might gain a bigger salary or power base.

The good news paradox also has a dangerous impact on a corporate level.

At our company I've always said that we would be better off looking at our profitable ventures and trying to make them more profitable. But it doesn't seem to work that way.

Let's say we produce a sports event and project it to show a $50,000 profit. Let's also say that we miss the projection by a mile. The event loses $5,000. That kind of bad news gets everyone's attention. They get very aggressive about cutting costs in every area—everything from using fewer people to run the event to using a lesser quality of paper in the souvenir program.

To me, these are all the areas we should be aggressively examining anyway. But there's the paradox. We only look at them when things go bad—when the event loses money—not when it shows a profit.

The most worrisome paradox of good news and its true relevance to decision making is that it often deludes managers into thinking that they are doing better in some areas of their business than they really are. Attractive numbers, in the form of rising sales and profits, often mask serious problems.

Some years back our company had to deal with a European executive in Tokyo who was running the Japanese operation of a luxury-goods company. I met him a few times and wasn't particularly impressed. I also received reports from our people there that he was something of a rogue manager. He spent money like a drunken sailor.

This didn't seem to bother his superiors. The Japanese were snapping up his company's products and he was turning in brilliant numbers. Of course, the numbers masked the fact that, in a surging Japanese economy, a child could have gone over there and done as well. The company was getting so much good news from Japan that they never bothered to look at how much money their man was spending or examine his business practices. It took his bosses at headquarters ten years—and a downturn in the local economy—to realize what an incompetent he was.

The bosses were so dazzled by the good news coming out of Tokyo that they couldn't conceive that there was any bad news.

THE ART OF CHANGING YOUR MIND

A friend of mine, the owner of a mid-sized sales organization, once got into a heated dispute over company strategy with one of his most valuable lieutenants. He had vetoed the lieutenant's proposal to invest more money in a pet project. The argument got intense and personal, to the point where my friend told the subordinate that if he didn't like it he ought to quit—which he did. My friend mentioned it to me the other day because he had second thoughts about the whole affair.

"Everybody in the company told me I was a fool to let him go," he said. "Now I realize they were right and I was wrong, not only to let him get away but to hold back money from his project. It was a good idea."

His problem, it turned out, was that he wanted to ask his lieutenant back, but he was afraid that reversing himself would make him look weak.

I've always wondered why bosses think they appear fickle and weak when they change their minds. I actually think it enhances their image as smart decision makers. I also think it generates respect rather than derision from the troops, particularly if the boss is correcting a patently bad decision.

Over the years I have made many blanket pronouncements in response to demands from our senior managers. If they're urging me to invest in a new area, I've stopped them in their tracks by saying things like, "We will never get into that business!" At the time, I meant it and I had my reasons. The timing wasn't right. I didn't like the people involved. The opportunity was too rich for my blood. Then, two years later, I changed my mind and got into the business I swore I would avoid. Again, I had my reasons, usually because the timing, personalities, and costs were more to my liking.

What I remember most about every time I reverse myself is that no one calls me on it. If they remember my grand pronouncement from two years earlier, they're not throwing it in my face. I suspect they're too busy being grateful that I'm finally endorsing their idea.

How did you feel the last time someone above you did a complete about-face—from disagreeing to agreeing with your proposal? I doubt if you thought, "Finally, the boss admits he was wrong!" More likely, you thought, "Finally, the boss thinks I'm right."

That's an important distinction. When you reverse your position, people usually don't think *what it says about you*. They're thinking *what it means for them*.

Gracefully executing a managerial flipflop and landing on your feet calls for some artistry, some mastery of subtle details. Here are four elements in the Art of Changing Your Mind:

1. LET SOME TIME GO BY.

There's nothing wrong with changing your mind, even from one minute to the next, if you do so because someone has filled in the blanks. But you should be alert to the time such a change takes.

As a general rule, you should give yourself as much time as possible between taking a position and reversing it. The more time goes by, the more likely that (a) circumstances will change to justify the reversal in everyone's eyes and (b) your employees will forget your original position.

It's one thing to take a position at the beginning of a meeting and then, for no apparent reason, reverse yourself at meeting's end. It is easy for me to see how people might regard that as flaky.

It's another thing altogether to reverse yourself within the same meeting *because some new significant information was introduced during that hour.* That's not fickle or weak. That's smart.

The artistic touch comes in when you delay the flipflop until some time after the meeting. There have been times when my associates have literally turned me around on a "firm" position during the course of a meeting. But I don't tell them that. I wait a few days or even a few weeks. I like the extra time to mull it over or discuss it with colleagues who have no stake in the decision.

I'm also aware of the cosmetics: The more time goes by before I announce my new position, the more considered, decisive, and final it appears. If I let enough time go by, sometimes it doesn't even look like a reversal. It's simply a new policy.

2. HAVE A FEW GOOD REASONS.

The more reasons you can articulate for changing your mind, the less whimsical and arbitrary that reversal will seem.

That should be obvious to anyone. Yet managers constantly reverse themselves purely on the basis of instinct or whimsy and think they can get away with it. If subordinates question them on the change, their only answer is, "Because I said so!" or "That's the way I want it." That's not decisive or commanding; it's merely bossy.

As a general rule, if you can't explain a change of mind to yourself, you probably can't explain it to your people. If you can't explain it to them, don't change it until you can.

3. BE CONFIDENT, EVEN WHEN YOU AREN'T.

When Ralph Houk was managing the New York Yankees in 1973, he chose the young, relatively unproven Graig Nettles as his everyday third baseman over the popular incumbent, Celerino Sanchez. Nettles was your typical "promising" player at the time, acquired from the Cleveland Indians after the 1972 season, but nowhere near the slick-fielding power hitter he would eventually become. Nettles got off to a horrible start in 1973, both in the field and at the plate. It didn't take much time before the fans and the press began to question Houk's confidence in Nettles and clamor for a change. But if Houk had doubts about Nettles's potential, he never showed them.

When a reporter asked him how long he was going to stay with Nettles, Houk replied, "I'm going to play him every day until he starts hitting, and then I'm going to play him because he's hitting."

A decision is more likely to stick in people's minds if you make it with supreme confidence and never reveal your doubts. That's even more true when you reverse yourself.

4. RESERVE THE RIGHT TO BE ARBITRARY.

There will always be situations when a manager must reverse himself but can't hide behind the subtle tactics enumerated above. He can't delay the decision. He can't come up with a list of good reasons. He can't improve the situation by stonewalling or feigning confidence.

At those times I invoke my right to be arbitrary. I know that our executives will balk at my new position because it doesn't seem fair or because it violates long-held assumptions about how our company works. But I have my reasons.

I may know certain facts that totally alter the face of a situation, yet the time has not come to share these facts with others.

I may have to make a decision that is good for the long-term interests of the entire company but seems to penalize parts of the company in the short run.

I may base the new position purely on speculation, on the fact that we may or may not be doing something in the future but need the new position to maintain that option.

In those moments, invoking the right to be arbitrary is the only way I can make a decision that seems neither popular, fair, nor easily understood.

In effect, I am asking our people to trust me. If I have employed the first three tactics well in the past and invoked the right to be arbitrary sparingly, gaining that trust shouldn't be a problem.

THE MOST DANGEROUS ASSUMPTION

The most dangerous assumption in business is that things will stay the same. Your customers will stay the same; they won't outgrow you. Your clients will stay the same; they won't move on without you. Your competitors will stay the same; they'll march in place while you move forward.

Obviously, effective managers and entrepreneurs know this is not true. They know that recognizing change and reacting to it quickly is the key to success, especially in the late 1990s when supersonic change is the only certainty we have.

Obvious as this may be, I'm always struck by how people forget the factor of change when it comes to making decisions. The same people who know that they must adapt constantly in order to keep pace with their customers and rivals somehow suspend that judgment when it comes to making informed decisions.

They'll dismiss an idea by saying, "We tried that five years ago and it was a disaster." For the purposes of making a decision, they assume that everything remains the same. They forget that the circumstances which may have made the idea "ahead of its time" five years ago may have altered sufficiently so the same idea is now "timely."

Conversely, they'll move forward with an idea, contending that "It worked five years ago. It should work again." Again, they assume that the world stands still. Tried and true ideas usually end up as tired and dead ideas if you make that false assumption.

I was reminded of this by Julian Bach, the head of our IMG Bach Literary Agency, who told me this story. When he was a young reporter at *Life* magazine after World War II, Julian was having lunch with a Romanian refugee who had fled the Nazis. The young man was struggling for a living in New York City, selling souvenir programs at the old Metropolitan Opera House when the great impresario Sol Hurok was producing ballets there.

It was a perfect Tuesday night in May. The Met was sold out. Two great stars were dancing. The young man sold most of his programs.

The next week, again Tuesday night, with the same perfect weather, the same two stars performing the same ballet, and the same sold-out Met, he hardly sold a program.

The doors closed. The curtain went up. Hurok and the refugee were alone in the lobby. Showing Hurok the unsold programs, the young man said he had no idea how to explain it.

Hurok said, "It's simple."

"What do you mean, simple!" said the refugee, clearly annoyed.

Hurok said, "It's a different Tuesday."

Keep this in mind the next time a client or boss or colleague shoots down your idea because *it's the same as a previous failure* or supports an idea because *it's the same as a previous success*. Whenever you hear someone in business say, "It's the same," count on it: They're wrong. It's always a different Tuesday.

BEWARE THE SPECTER OF PERFECT MATH

In my previous book, *On Negotiating*, I described two associates discussing cost-cutting in our New York operation. The item at hand was an apartment we keep for visiting clients. One associate contended that we could make money on the apartment if, as she said, "we could put a client in the apartment every week of the year and charge them $500 per week. Multiply that by fifty-two weeks and the $26,000 would cover the rent." She used the same calculus for several other items, to the point where the apartment looked like a potential profit center.

An associate cut her off, saying, "That sounds good, but you're using perfect math. I seriously doubt if the apartment will be full each week."

I liked that phrase, "perfect math," because it summed up all the false or inflated assumptions that pollute our decision making each day. I think we're all guilty of perfect math in one way or another when we start off with an attractive number or fact and use that as the basis for an uninterrupted chain of events to achieve a stated goal. The truth is that it usually doesn't work out that way. Even if we start off with fairly sound assumptions, things rarely fall into place as neatly as we would like them to.

Like the best negotiators, the best decision makers are always vigilant for signs of perfect math—in themselves as well as others—and they use these signs to improve, not cloud, their judgment.

Perfect math rears its pernicious head most obviously with budgets and projections.

Basically, people deal with projections in three ways.

There are the eternal optimists who continually overestimate future earnings and thus always fall short of their goals.

There are the eternal pessimists who continually lowball their projections so they can exceed their goals at year's end and look like heroes.

And then there are the people who almost always hit their projections right on target.

Obviously, the people who hit their targets year in and year out have the keenest appreciation of the dangers of perfect math. They know all the variables that can puncture holes in their assumptions—and they allow for them.

Equally obvious is that the eternal optimists don't appreciate the dangers of perfect math. For whatever reason, they're addicted to making pie-in-the-sky assumptions and their performance reflects this.

Less obvious is how dangerous the eternal pessimists can be. They're also guilty of perfect math; the only difference is that their numbers are too conservative rather than too liberal. I've learned over the years, however, that an overly modest projection is just as bad for managing a company as a projection that is too ambitious.

I can understand why people make modest projections. If they secretly hope to show a $100,000 profit next year and project $10,000, they look like heroes when the actual number comes in at $80,000. They don't realize that if the company planned its expansion, its hiring, its new offices, and its cash flow based on that $10,000, the company would never grow.

A good manager corrects his people not only for promising too much but for aiming too low.

MOTIVATE WITH PERFECT MATH

The one good thing about perfect math is that it can be a great motivational tool. Although as a manager I don't want to base my decisions on inflated numbers, that hasn't stopped me from inflating targets to prod people to do better.

If a subordinate is falling short of expectations on, say, selling a golf instructional video, I'm not above using the same perfect math that the golf inventor used on me. I can hear myself saying, "You mean to tell me that with ten million avid golfers out there, we can't get 100,000 of them—that's a measly 1 percent—to pay $19.95 for this video?" If nothing else, they leave my office with an expanded sense of the video's potential and my expectations.

Perfect math may be a lousy way to make decisions, but it can be downright inspirational when you want people to try harder.

• • •
THE McCORMACK RULES

- Being an entrepreneur (or any type of manager) is a lifelong, humbling process of learning when to go with your gut and when to go with something more real.

- Instinct is not a perfect science; it's not even an imperfect science. It's an art form.

- If there is no void to fill, don't rush in.

- The biggest reason people make too many gut decisions is that other people force them into it.

- The paradox of good news is that it often blinds us to the bad news.

- Good managers who treat hiring decisions casually will soon be rotten managers.

- There's a difference between having an ego and having an ego problem.

- The more reasons you can articulate for changing your mind, the less arbitrary that reversal will seem. As a general rule, if you can't explain a change of mind to yourself, you probably can't explain it to your people. If you can't explain it to them, don't change it until you can.

- A decision is more likely to stick in people's minds if you make it with supreme confidence and never reveal your doubts. That's even more true when you reverse yourself.

- The most dangerous assumption in business is that things will stay the same.

- A good manager corrects his people not only for promising too much but for aiming too low.

CHAPTER 6

Making Meetings
Matter More

WHEN IN DOUBT, DON'T
CALL A MEETING

Everyone knows the standard advice for getting the most out of meetings. Start promptly. Have a specific agenda. Don't leave the room without deciding something, anything (even if it's nothing more than scheduling the next time you meet).

It's hard to argue with this advice once you've assembled employees for a meeting. But it doesn't address the question of whether you should have called the meeting in the first place. Here are five questions to ask yourself *before* you call a meeting to order:

1. If you have an opening in your schedule, do you call a meeting? Bosses don't call meetings out of malice. Sometimes they call them out of habit. To them, meetings are what you do

when there's nothing else to do. This is not healthy for the organization. While the boss is filling up his time, he's wasting
that of his employees—and baffling them. There are many
reasons to schedule an internal meeting, but whim is not one
of them.

2. Can you say, "You're right. I never considered that."? Many
meetings drag on long beyond their usefulness because the
boss sees them as a forum for debate and rhetoric. The boss uses
meetings to hand down edicts, not to encourage solutions
from the troops. The boss must always prevail. Is it any wonder that such meetings tend to demoralize rather than inspire
the attendees? Don't call a meeting unless you have mastered
the ability to say "You're right," without worrying that it also
means "I'm wrong."

3. Are there certain people whose ideas you automatically resist?
Many meetings founder when the boss takes too much time arguing over minor details. Quite often, these little arguments
take place between the boss and the same two or three people. Ask yourself: Is it the person or the concept that I don't
like? If it's the former, you won't solve your problem by calling a meeting.

4. Are you too comfortable? Some bosses regard meetings as a
treat, a respite from their real job. They call for refreshments,
lean back in their chair, prop up their feet, and encourage
everyone to make themselves at home. This may be one reason why some meetings take so long to go nowhere. Everyone
is too comfortable. There's no incentive to make the meeting
end. One solution: Meet in a neutral site, with wooden chairs
or none at all.

5. How honest are you and how honest do you want everyone else to be? The only thing worse than getting no answers in a meeting is getting patently false ones. You see this among employees afflicted with "Let's not bother the boss" syndrome—where employees only relate good news to the boss, even though the bad news is infinitely more important. Before you call a meeting, make sure you're prepared for the worst and that your associates are instructed to tell you as much.

HOW TRADITION CAN STRANGLE YOUR MEETINGS

There's a lot to be said for tradition in any organization. Whether they take the form of an annual picnic for employees and family members or a week-long retreat for senior management each May or the CEO dressing up as Santa Claus at Christmas, traditions are the lifeblood of an organization. They give it character and stability.

However, there is one feature of organizational life where I think managers would benefit from ignoring rather than adhering to tradition. I'm talking about meetings.

Tradition is the bane of effective meetings. As a CEO, I probably spend more time thinking about the makeup, timing, length, and form of our company's various meetings than I do about any other managerial responsibility.

My biggest fear is that we will get in a meetings rut.

I noticed this not long ago with our tennis division meetings. When the division was one-tenth the size it is now, traditionally the big annual tennis meeting would start at a given hour and end at a given hour on a specific day in August when everyone would be in New York for the U.S. Open. Within that time frame we could cover everything we had to cover. The group was small enough to make the meeting substantive and meaningful. Everyone had a chance to contribute or get embroiled in intelligent exchanges. Plus, every topic at the meeting was of direct interest to everyone present.

But as the tennis division grew in personnel and in complexity—as it expanded beyond the traditional management of tennis players into areas such as events, products, resort facilities, and tennis academies—the annual meeting's structure and length remained the same. Unfortunately, the allotted time was not sufficient to adequately cover the new areas. Not only was there not enough time, but the time itself was a waste for many people. As an interested observer, I would find myself listening to a half-hour discussion among four people that left the remaining thirty-six people twiddling their thumbs. They were not interested in the discussion. They couldn't contribute. They couldn't even learn from it. In short, tradition had rendered the meeting unwieldy and counterproductive.

My recommendation to all managers is simple: If you have a volatile, dynamic, ever-changing company or division, you must periodically rip apart the complete fabric of your meetings. Question every aspect of the meeting—the agenda, the format, the length, the locale, the cast of characters— and be particularly ruthless with those features that exist solely because of historical precedent. When people justify a policy or practice because "We've always done it this way," a good manager knows precisely where to start slashing.

Here are three factors that meeting leaders should always be questioning.

1. THE CAST OF CHARACTERS.

The most hidebound aspect of any meeting is the cast of characters.

It's difficult to shrink the size of a meeting. If one year I ask ten people to come to London to review our real estate projects, those same ten people will expect to be invited the following year. In their mind they are charter members of the "real estate committee." And they will go through some incredible machinations to ensure that they are invited to the next meeting.

The trap here, of course, is that our real estate meetings are doomed to always get bigger—and progressively less productive. In the second year, three new people may join the original ten attendees. In the third year, perhaps another two people join the now-traditional thirteen. A good manager recognizes this trap and is constantly reassessing who should attend and who should not. Disinviting a few people may seem rude, but to the people in the meeting it is the highest compliment—because the manager is respecting their time.

2. THE FORMAT.

The format of a meeting is another feature that is often damaged rather than improved by tradition.

I know one executive who runs all his quarterly division meetings exactly the same way. He opens the meeting with a few quick remarks, asks his second-in-command if she has anything to report, and then goes around the table so everyone gets a hearing. His agenda, in effect, is the seating chart.

Another executive does the opposite. He dominates his meetings by talking for hours and then, with the clock winding down, asks people to comment.

I know for a fact that meetings run by these two executives are dreaded events—because they are so predictable. In the first example, the attendees know they will be called on to speak, so they prepare a statement—even though many have nothing valuable to say. In the other example, the attendees are equally dispirited because they know they will never get a fair hearing to present their case.

I suspect that most executives have a set pattern for running a meeting. Some are dominators. Some function as referees while others do the talking. Some like to instigate conflicts and see how they are resolved.

Think about your style of running a meeting. Do you go into every meeting with the same tired approach? Would people walk into—and out of—your meetings with greater enthusiasm if you tried something different?

3. THE TIME.

The toughest meeting habit to break is probably its length. The weekly Monday morning staff meeting that's scheduled from nine o'clock to twelve will always take three hours, whether there's a full agenda on some mornings or very little to discuss on others. Why? Because people think of it as a three-hour meeting and (in mass allegiance to Parkinson's Law) adjust their behavior, pace, and comments to fill up the allotted time.

It's no different with the all-day monthly sales meeting or the quarterly get-together of your senior managers. If attendees know the meeting traditionally lasts eight hours, its length is a self-fulfilling prophecy.

The irony here is that time is probably the easiest feature to control in a meeting—if you do your homework before you meet.

I always have an agenda before I go into a meeting. I don't necessarily broadcast it to the attendees or, as some executives like to do, distribute it in writing as people enter the room. But I do give it a lot of thought. If I have thirty-five points to cover, I treat each point like an accountant with his ledger. I gauge how much time we need to discuss each point. I then factor in some time for digressions. If it is a meeting with senior executives, who tend to be more loquacious and forthcoming with their opinions, I ask them ahead of time what points they want to add to the agenda and how much time they think they'll need. Totaling up my estimates tells me how long the meeting should last.

It also tells me how to prioritize my thirty-five points. As a general rule, I like to deal with the quick, easy points on my agenda first and tackle the meatier issues last. Experience has taught me that it's better to have covered thirty-four points and be in a long discussion at the end that I can terminate for another time than to have the long discussion first and not be able to cover, say, twenty-one of the remaining thirty-four points.

Incredibly, I know a lot of managers who do this backwards. They call a four-hour meeting and hope they can squeeze their thirty-five points in. Thus, when they get bogged down in a forty-five-minute digression on one point, they're not aware that they have only 195 minutes left to cover thirty-four points, or about five minutes a point. If they did the arithmetic, they'd realize that's not enough time.

What's irritating to me when I've sat in on meetings like this is not that we shouldn't be spending forty-five minutes on one subject. That's all right. But why schedule a meeting for four hours solely out of habit when a little forethought will tell you that you really need eight?

BE GRATEFUL THAT YOUR PEOPLE DISAGREE

The CEO of a mid-sized company described a situation to me that probably sends a tremor of recognition into the heart of any entrepreneur.

He had just come out of an all-day internal meeting that was frighteningly calm and free of rancor. I remember he specifically used the word "frightening" because he couldn't help thinking that some of the people in the room surely must have disagreed with the decisions made in the meeting but were unwilling or afraid to say so. He thought it was a scary situation and wondered what he could do to encourage a little more dissent and free-wheeling debate.

He was right to be worried. I'd much rather have a company where everyone disagreed some of the time than a company where everyone agreed all of the time. Total agreement is not healthy. Even the Japanese, who are obsessed with building consensus among co-workers, arrive at that harmony only through a lively (but dignified) process of debate and disagreement.

Here are two suggestions—one personal, the other in-stitutional—that can create a healthy culture of dissent at any company.

1. THE OUTRAGEOUS OPINION.

A wise man once told me his biggest fear as a boss was not knowing who the "yes men" were on his staff and who would tell him the unvarnished truth. "The day I can't tell the dif-ference is the day I'm finished," he said.

So he would periodically toss out outrageous opinions designed to test the character of his associates. He would chal-lenge a subordinate's ideas, even if he privately agreed with them, saying, "You don't know what you're talking about!" If the subordinate stood his ground, that told him something positive about that individual. If he backed down, that told him something else.

"It's the Emperor's Clothes syndrome," he said. "I know there are people who think I'm out of my mind for some of the things I say. But when I'm wrong, I want people to tell me so."

If you want your people to be a little more combative with each other, you may have to throw the first punches.

2. THE DISSENTING OPINION.

When the nine Supreme Court justices vote 6-3 on a case, they deliver their verdict in a majority opinion which decides the case but also publish the opinions of the three dissenters. Legals scholars will tell you that some of the most interesting ideas can be found in the dissenting opinion.

175

Some companies use a variation of this system to encourage debate and air out wild ideas. At Motorola, for example, each employee is entitled to file a "minority report" if he
feels his ideas aren't being given a fair shake. These reports
aren't simply filed away or smothered by the employee's boss.
On the contrary, they are reviewed by the boss's superior and
openly discussed. Taking any sort of vindictive action against
the author of a "minority report" is considered cowardly.

I'm not sure if this system can work at every company.
You certainly don't want to create a culture where people are
obsessed with putting every thought in writing and entering
it into some official record. They're better off doing their job.
But if you want healthy disagreement, you have to give people a way to be heard and you have to assure them that they
won't be punished for being different. The dissenting opinion
seems to fit the bill.

Ordering Events to Your Advantage

I'm convinced that most people don't give enough thought
to the power of sequence—the order in which they allow information to be exposed in a public forum—in their business
dealings.

If they're running a meeting, they don't think about
whom they will call on first and whom last.

If they're making a progress report to their boss, they
don't stop to consider which achievements they should lead
off with and which to hold until the end.

If they're presenting a list of ideas in a sales presentation, they don't organize the list in a sequence that will make their gems shine and their throwaways disappear.

Yet paying attention to the sequence of events in any of these three situations is incredibly simple—and the payoff can be considerable.

I recall a meeting in our London office a few years ago that illustrates how simple it is to order events to your advantage—and the blunt power when you do it with a little imagination.

A rift had developed in our London operations between our television division and the rest of IMG. The TV group had become very successful and had begun to think of itself as a force apart from the core of our company. This prima donna attitude was largely being promoted by the man running our TV division, and it threatened the integrity of the London office.

I called a meeting to patch up the situation. All of our European TV sales and production people gathered in a conference room, where I was prepared to discuss a long list of grievances and, if necessary, lay down the law to the group on the need for intracorporate cooperation.

But I abandoned this agenda as soon as I looked at the seating arrangement in the room and noted that the renegade head of the TV division was seated to my immediate left.

So I made a short speech about my vision of the organization and how I expected them to behave. And then I asked each of them, "Do you understand that you are working for IMG, not the television division, and your priorities should reflect that? Just give me a simple yes or no."

I started with the person on my immediate right and went around the room in order. One by one, each employee answered "yes," they agreed with my decision. As the "yes's" mounted up, we finally came to the division head, who sat there stunned and enraged.

To his credit, he stuck to his guns. He said, "No."

But I could see that this bit of "theater" had shaken him up considerably and established to everyone in the room how clearly out of sync he was with his people and our company. That was the beginning of the end for him at our company. I doubt if that meeting would have been as quick, painless, and effective if I had posed my question to him first instead of last.

Controlling the sequence of events in a meeting doesn't have to be as theatrical as this episode from my past. In fact, the power of ordering things your way is far greater if you downplay it, if people aren't aware of it.

Let's say I'm going into a meeting with a client to review our activities on his behalf. We have twenty-five subjects to discuss. That's a long agenda. Let's also say I'm nervous about one or two items on the agenda. I'm not happy about what we accomplished in those areas.

If I can control the agenda, it would be foolish for me to start off the meeting with those negatives. It opens me up to criticism, puts me on the defensive, and can negatively color the rest of the meeting. Yet it amazes me how often people do start off meetings with "First, the bad news . . ."—as if getting the negatives out of the way will ensure smooth sailing the rest of the way. It never does.

Instead, I make a point of preceding the negative item with three or four items where we have done mindblowing work. That gives me the confidence to say, "You've just heard what we did for you in Australia. You've heard about the tremendous deal in France. And here's that $100,000 royalty check from Canada. Now, here's a project in Spain where, frankly, we didn't do so well."

That cushions the blow. Given all we've done for the client in Australia, France, and Canada, he might be more forgiving of our trespasses in Spain. What makes this even more attractive from my standpoint is that the client is probably not aware of all the strings I've pulled so he would come to that conclusion.

It's the same with selling ideas to your boss or customer. If you have a shopping list of twenty ideas, four of which are genuinely good and the rest are not so good, in what sequence do you present them?

Some people start off with the best ideas and work their way down. I think this is bad because, among other things, it ends the meeting on a low note.

Some people reverse this, ranking the ideas from bad to good and working their way up to a strong finish. Of course, they also run the risk of losing their audience's interest before they get to the grand finale.

They're thinking about sequence, but not wisely. I would prefer to mix it up. I would lead off with two or three weak ideas and then hit my audience with a strong one—and continue that pattern throughout the meeting. A good idea, I've found, is always more appealing if it is preceded by a poor one.

If people don't give enough thought to the sequence of *what* is discussed in a meeting, they're even worse about *who* discusses it. You can gain a lot by controlling the order of people you call on in a meeting.

If you think you are going to get some negative feedback on an issue that you want positively resolved in a meeting, you're much better off calling first on people who you know will favor your point of view. You pick your advocates. If you think Joe, Tom, Beth, Susan, and Bill are on your side and Tony isn't, by all means call on those five people first. Getting five yeas on an issue might negate whatever impassioned plea Tony may make for his point of view.

If you are really a master of sequencing things to your advantage, you might even find yourself lobbying Joe, Tom, Beth, Susan, and Bill before the meeting and telling them what you plan to do.

NEVER BRING THE PROBLEMS OF ONE MEETING TO THE NEXT

In my early years, when I first started traveling to Europe regularly on business, I happened to be on a New York-to-London flight sitting next to a young television executive with an avid interest in golf. We became friendly, and met a few times to discuss possible projects. But he was always telling me, "You really ought to meet my chairman. He loves golf and can do a lot for you and the sport."

Actually, I was well aware of his chairman. If I had a top ten list of chief executives I most wanted to meet, this particular boss was near the top. An introductory meeting was set up by my new friend for my next visit to London. At the appointed hour, I showed up at the chairman's imposing headquarters. My friend met me in the lobby and walked me to the chairman's office, where a secretary informed us that the chairman was running a few minutes behind schedule. My friend and I returned to his office and whiled away the time with small talk. After fifteen minutes, with the small talk exhausted, my friend was getting a little edgy. This meeting was as big a deal to him as it was to me. He called the chairman's secretary to remind her that we were waiting.

Another fifteen minutes passed. My friend called again. Finally, we were ushered into the great man's office. He couldn't have been more gracious or charming. I had hoped for three minutes to say hello and he gave me thirty minutes, during which he described ways we could work together in golf and encouraged me to contact him directly any time I had an appropriate idea. I had no idea what sort of emergency had detained him and kept us waiting, and if he was agitated or distracted, he gave no indication of it in our meeting.

I later learned that just before my arrival that morning several members of the chairman's management team had abruptly resigned (with the blessing of some disgruntled board members). My friend and I were kept waiting because the chairman was holed up in his office lining up board members to fight off a palace coup. He was caught up in a major crisis, but when he met with me, I didn't have a clue!

The man was a master at compartmentalizing. He knew instinctively that you shouldn't take the problems of one meeting (no matter how grave or disturbing) into the next meeting. If you can't do that, you might as well cancel the next meeting—because you won't be functioning at your best. If you're upset, you might irritate the other people at the meeting. If you're distracted, you might confuse them.

I suspect the chairman's golf experience may have had something to do with it. Golfers are taught early on that it's dangerous to let poor play on one hole affect their play on the next hole. You have to shrug it off and move on as if it never happened. That's easier said than done in golf, where the slightest loss of confidence and concentration can throw off your game. But the perennial champions seem to do it with remarkable consistency. The champions in business can do it as well. No matter how distressing the details of one situation may be, they can shrug it off, regroup emotionally, and approach the next event with a clean slate.

The ability to compartmentalize is even more valuable once you appreciate how inadequate most people in business are in this regard. A person who lets his emotions—good or bad—spill over from one situation to the next is a sitting duck for anyone who has control of his or her emotions and has given some thought to how he or she wants to arrange a certain sequence of events.

For example, some years ago I had to regularly deal with an executive who was notorious for being an emotional powderkeg. This rampant emotionalism often served him well. When things were going his way, he could be incredibly clever, dynamic, and generous. When his spirits were high, he could literally carry an entire division of staffers with his energy and enthusiasm. When things turned sour, he tended to be incredibly argumentative and unyielding. Obviously, if I wanted something from him, it was important to catch him when he was on a roll.

Over time I learned that I could maneuver him into one state or the other within the span of a single meeting simply by ordering the sequence of topics to my advantage. Whenever I needed a big block of his time, his wisdom, and his undivided attention, I always armed myself with one or two upbeat bulletins to open the discussion. To kick off the meeting with bad news would have been disastrous. He would become sullen and totally unhelpful.

I'm not sure he realizes how manipulable he is. But that's one of the bonuses of learning to compartmentalize. Once you see it in yourself, you begin to see its presence or absence in others.

HOW TO FORM A COMMITTEE THAT WORKS

If people say they hate meetings, they probably feel even more strongly about committees. Committees, like meetings, have taken an unfair beating in recent years—mostly because so many executives don't know how to make a committee work.

They form too many committees.

They put the wrong people on it.

They don't give the committee a clear mandate.

They ignore or overrule the committee's decisions.

I have formed (and disbanded) my share of committees at our company over the years. Some were successful, some were not, but cumulative experience has taught me a few rules about what makes a committee work. Here are five all managers need to consider before their committee's first session:

1. MAKE A STATEMENT.

Committees are usually formed to solve a problem. That in itself is the best feature of a committee: It makes a statement.

It lets you announce to everyone in the company that a problem exists, that you take it seriously, and that you intend to
correct it.

Don't squander this opportunity to make a statement by
forming your committee in relative silence. Announce it publicly. Distribute a memo to everyone in your organization
about the committee—who is on it, why it's being formed,
and what you expect it to accomplish. Broadcasting the committee's existence not only focuses attention on the problem,
but it focuses attention on the committee members and challenges them to do more than just talk.

2. ELIMINATE THE ELITIST ELEMENT.

The normal impulse in forming a committee is to stack it with
senior people, to form a "blue ribbon" committee that is the
be-all and end-all of decision-making bodies.

There are several things wrong with this approach.

First, from a practical standpoint, an elite committee is
harder to convene on a regular basis. Your most senior people
are probably your busiest people. They travel the most, they
have the most crowded calendars, and they have the most
projects demanding their attention. If you've ever found it
difficult to organize a meeting with one busy executive, imagine what you'll have to go through to get six busy people in the
same room several times a year.

Second, an elite committee tends to be self-congratula-
tory and self-sustaining. Everyone looks around the room the
first day, assessing the rank of the other members and congratulating themselves on being among such a high-powered

group. The committee may not get much done, but everyone will be so pleased to be a part of this august "club" that they will never move to disband it.

Third, an elite committee tends to breed resentment—by the people who have not been included in this prestigious group.

3. PICK CREDIBLE PEOPLE.

In my mind, the most important factor in who you put on a committee is how much credibility each member gives you with the various constituencies in your company that will be affected by the committee.

For example, several years ago we formed an administrative operations committee in our company as a layer between our financial people and our line executives. This committee's mandate is to review all administrative and operating expenses and to recommend policies that are more cost-effective for our various North American offices.

On first glance, the committee seemed like a motley crew. There were representatives from all levels in the company. Some employees were puzzled by my seemingly random selection of committee members, but the group's makeup was something I gave a lot of thought to.

I wanted an executive from our events group, to get the support of our event organizers and stop them from accusing us of not knowing the "real world" problems they face every week.

I put on an executive from our Boston office, who could speak for our various small- to mid-size satellite branches. I put on an accounting person, who had the support of our chief financial officer.

I put on an attorney who was familiar with the legal issues of operating several facilities and dealing with contractors and suppliers.

I also put on an office manager and a secretary to provide credibility with our non-executive staff.

The point is that you don't need senior people to make a committee work. You can have people of all ranks as long as they have credibility with the senior people they work for.

4. Don't tolerate no-shows.

If a committee is really important, don't let anyone get away with not attending. It is better to postpone a session than to meet with one or two constituencies missing. Someone will always accuse you of railroading a decision through in their absence.

5. Shock the system quickly.

As a general rule, if a committee has done nothing substantive in the first two or three months that it can put down in writing and distribute throughout the company, then it has failed.

A committee's first decision is its most important one. That's where it announces its intentions—if it is serious about the problem or just going through the motions. So make sure that your first decision shocks the system.

• • •

THE McCORMACK RULES

- If you have a volatile, dynamic, ever-changing company or division, you must periodically rip apart the complete fabric of your meetings.

- The only thing worse than getting no answers in a meeting is getting patently false ones.

- Before you call a meeting, make sure you're prepared for the worst and that your associates are instructed to tell you as much.

- Don't call a meeting unless you have mastered the ability to say "You're right" without worrying that it also means "I'm wrong."

- When people justify a policy or practice because "We've always done it this way," a good manager knows precisely where to start slashing.

- If you want your people to be a little more combative with each other, you may have to throw the first punches.

- If a committee is really important, don't let anyone get away with not attending.

CHAPTER 7

Cutting Costs

WELCOME TO THE "NEW AUSTERITY"

The owner of a small but successful sales organization approached me once after a speech to discuss how difficult it was to cut costs at his company. In the past, when the economic picture was rosier, he and his salespeople tended to be rather careless about expenses. Profits were skyrocketing. Money was no object. Now, he was learning, the company had to watch every penny.

"It's not easy getting the troops to switch from a first-class lifestyle to coach," he told me. "They don't seem to believe in our new austerity. They think it applies to everyone else, not them."

I'm sure this entrepreneur wasn't alone in his concerns. It's tough to make a sudden U-turn in everyday business practices, especially when changing those practices seems painful to your most valuable people. Like many owners and managers, this man was struggling to cut costs without demoralizing his people.

In a way, I'm not the right person to look to for sympathy—because I have always been a fanatic about expenses. I've never thought employees should use the company to subsidize their first-class lifestyle, so I'm always looking out for signs of foolish or intemperate spending. And I don't let these signs pass without comment. Here are four suggestions that can help any manager introduce his troops to the "new austerity."

1. SELECTIVE MONITORING.

Our company has grown well beyond the point where I can (or even want to) keep an eye on every expense in every one of our seventy offices around the world. But I can pick my spots. I can have our financial people audit a certain type of expenditure and if we find something outrageous, I can make our people aware of it. My favorite sort of excess is the small, nitpicky item that no one thinks we would bother to examine—because it gets people thinking: If we're looking at the little items, we're certainly looking at the big ones.

At a certain point in the growth of any company, the boss can't personally keep track of every expense. But your people can't be sure of that.

2. HORROR STORIES.

I like to make my points with horror stories. If I announce at a meeting, "We are not reviewing our expenses carefully," that's not a very strong statement. Everyone will yawn and think, "Oh no, not again." The point will make no impression.

But if I can cite specific examples of excess, that's a different story.

For example, we urge all our American executives traveling in Europe to use USA Direct when calling the U.S. By dialing seven extra digits they save our company a lot of money. To see how people were complying with this, we audited the telephone expenses of our tennis executives at a European tournament. We learned that, had they used USA Direct, they would have saved $800 on international phone calls. So I pointed this out in a meeting. Doing so delivers more than one message. It not only highlights the specific savings but it shows that we're watching everything. The benefit is exponential. Everyone in the company eventually gets the message, not just the people in the room but the people who report to them. And the message doesn't only refer to USA Direct.

3. More horror stories.

I also tend to go overboard on the horror stories. If I have ten stories, I use them all. I don't stop at story number three because I think our people get the message. I want to make the point that this is not nitpicking. I want them to know that it's serious, that this is how we run our business.

4. Head before the tail.

I also prefer to attack the head, not the tail of the problem. If a junior executive has some expense account irregularities, I won't personally chastise him for it. I'll chastise his boss, the senior executive who approved the irregularities. Again, that sends a double message. The senior executive will go back to his staff, embarrassed and contrite, and be more aggressive about getting everyone to toe the line.

If you want to stop the excesses at your company, first you have to identify them. Audit everyone's expenses and find as many horror stories as you can. Then show your people how they can do better.

If you want your people to take your "new austerity" seriously, start at the top. Cut your spending habits first. A cost-cutting program that starts from the bottom will not work. A program that starts at the top will not fail.

Four Things I Know About Downsizing

One of the tenets of being an entrepreneur is that you cannot be afraid of rapid growth. There are a lot of dangers with growing too fast—namely, the strain on your personnel, your finances, and your attention to detail—but an entrepreneur is generally willing to take the risk. If an opportunity presents itself, the entrepreneur bites into it—and worries about digesting it later.

The converse is also true. An entrepreneur cannot be afraid of rapid contraction. If a crisis comes up, he should be willing to cut—and worry about the payback later.

Unfortunately, downsizing is not an area where many entrepreneurs distinguish themselves. They cut too little or too late. They cut muscle, not fat. They resist cutting their "sacred cows." In many cases, they're incapable of making cuts at all.

This isn't surprising. The fearlessness you need to go into business for yourself is not the same as the courage you need to stay in business at all costs. (Some people can play offense but not defense.) Plus, the adrenaline rush of building a business is infinitely more pleasurable than the soul-searing pain of dismantling it. Thus, some managers get downsizing all wrong. Here are four bits of common sense I know about shrinking a business.

1. THE SECOND CUT IS THE DEEPEST.

The first round of cutbacks is usually the easiest (once employees get used to the idea). If management wants a sweeping 10 percent cut in expenses and head count, people can usually handle that. There's enough fat in most organizations to justify it.

It's the second round of cuts you have to watch. These are the cuts that managers resist. It's an interesting dynamic. Once executives cut, they think the process is over. They're reluctant to trim more budget or let more people go—in large part because of selfishness. They think, "If I lose these people, I'll never be able to hire new people once business picks up." As a result, a creeping paralysis settles into a downsizing operation because people are afraid of not being able to replace or rehire or get back what they have lost.

There's no easy cure for this sort of thinking, but telling your people that downsizing is not a permanent thing is a good place to start.

2. Downsize and upsize together.

In any vibrant company, you have to be downsizing and up-sizing at the same time. If two areas of your business are grow-ing despite a faltering economy and a lot of areas are in trouble, it's foolish to make cuts in the growth areas just be-cause you are cutting in the weak areas. All you're doing is eroding your power base.

Yet I can see how some organizations fall into this trap. If you tell the heads of six faltering divisions to cut 20 percent of their budget, they will want to know why you're singling them out, why you're not making the same demands of two other executives who are running thriving divisions. For the sake of corporate harmony, I can see where some managers would mandate cuts in the thriving divisions, too.

Of course, that's madness. While you're trimming the weak areas, you should be beefing up your strong areas.

If you position this process as a reallocation of corporate resources, it can actually provide a morale boost. Downsizings, by definition, are scary and demoralizing. When the layoffs and cutbacks come, that's all people talk about. No one talks about the hirings and expansion in other areas. But they should.

3. Threats get results.

People resist downsizing because it usually means hurting other people. If you tell executives to trim their T&E budget or cancel a major computer purchase, they can usually live with that. But if you ask them to let people go, that's a different form of bloodshed.

It's not just because firing someone is awkward for many people. It's also because letting people go raises doubts about a manager's judgment. Generally speaking, all managers believe their people are talented. That's why they hired them, promoted them, and gave them raises. In a downsizing it's tough for a manager to admit that people he has been praising for years are suddenly dispensable. It's a blow to his managerial acumen.

As a result, he is not the best person to decide which people to let go. He thinks all his people are great and everybody else's staff is disposable.

It would be fascinating to see the results if the head of Division A had to trim Division B's staff and vice versa. But that's not practical. My solution is to tone down that sort of threat. I give the managers a financial target and let them reach it as they see fit. But I always remind them, "If you don't make the cuts, I will." Managers, I've found, tend to respond quickly whenever you threaten to do something they know they should be doing themselves.

4. Downsizings are good for you.

This is the most interesting aspect of downsizings. In my experience, at least 80 percent of what a company does in a downsizing mode is what it should have done anyway.

A look at the business section of the newspaper will confirm this. Story after story describes how a company cut 2000 people and nothing bad happened or a company trimmed its sales force by 300 and still maintained its steady growth. When a large public company announces massive layoffs, investors generally say, "It's about time!"—and bid up the company's stock price.

That's the real secret about downsizings. They force you to look at costs that you should have been looking at all along.

You Can Never Stop Cutting Costs

The funny thing about building a business is that no matter how big you get or how successful you feel, you can never rest. You have to keep finding new customers, create new products, enter new territories, and bring fresh talent into your organization—all in the name of generating more revenues.

It's the same on the expense side of the ledger. You have to keep finding new ways to cut costs.

I used to be relatively lax about our company's operating costs. I didn't even have budgets for our line and staff divisions. I assumed our people were responsible and would spend whatever it took to get the job done. At the end of the year, we added up the bills and as long as our income exceeded our outgo, I figured we were doing all right.

But I noticed as the company grew, expenses had a pernicious tendency to outpace revenue. I'm not sure why this happens. Perhaps it was because we were so focused on sales that we forgot about costs. In the past several years, we've had a major attitude adjustment regarding costs. We regard every operating cost at every level of the company with suspicion. With a little imagination, we think every expense can be reduced. Here are some of my favorite cost cuts, which all managers can pursue at their companies, too.

1. The fax stamp.

The head of our Minneapolis office pointed out that the cover sheet on the majority of faxes we sent was a waste of paper and telephone time. People rarely put an important message on the cover sheet other than the self-evident "Please deliver to. . ." So we created a fax stamp that eliminated the need for a cover sheet. Now our people stamp the first page of their documents and write in the pertinent data (*i.e.*, name, date, fax number, number of pages). This suggestion saved us $40,000.

2. Fight the round bill.

Whenever I see a bill with more zeroes than numbers—whether it's $500 or $50,000—I question it. We had a meeting at a British resort for our European executives recently and the telephone charges for our group came to exactly 1500 pounds. That's a red flag to me. Something was wrong. The phone charges couldn't possibly come to 1500 pounds even. Somebody had rounded it off. So we asked the resort to break down all the phone bills—and it turned out that they had indeed added some long-distance surcharges to round off the bill.

I'm not suggesting that every round bill from every supplier is padded and that you should treat all vendors as adversaries. But 90 percent of the time when we investigate a bill that seems too even, we conclude that we were right and the other party was wrong.

3. BOOK AIR TRAVEL IN ADVANCE.

It doesn't take a genius to realize that advance-purchased airline tickets represent a big saving in travel costs. But it's sometimes hard to get that point across to employees.

So we instituted a mandatory three-day advance purchase policy on all airline travel. That doesn't mean we've eliminated emergency travel or don't recognize that some trips can't be planned ahead. But full-price tickets purchased under the three-day limit now require a senior manager's approval.

Most people are well-organized. They know where they have to be weeks ahead of time. And the airlines reward them for it. It's foolish for our company not to cash in on that reward.

4. MAKE PEOPLE PAY FOR PERSONAL CALLS.

Now that long-distance phone companies can provide data about every employee's monthly telephone usage, we expect our executives to review their phone bills and reimburse the company for any personal long-distance calls made during business hours. This isn't as draconian as it sounds. We don't enforce the policy; it's actually an honor system. But I'm heartened by the fact that most people do reimburse the company (the average check is $15). It means they're spending company money as if it were their own.

5. APPROVE OVERNIGHT COURIERS.

Overnight couriers are a luxury, not the standard operating procedure. They are also a dangerous sign of runaway costs at a company.

People have a tendency to overestimate rather than underestimate the urgency of the material they mail out. As a result, their judgment gets clouded on whether they should send a package via a next-day courier or regular mail will do. We want them to think more clearly about this decision.

So every overnight package we send out requires company approval. Adding that extra step of filling out the approval form makes people a little more thoughtful about whether their package absolutely, positively has to be there overnight. The annual savings to us are astounding.

6. MAKE THE RECIPIENT PAY FOR SPEED.

If someone wants a package delivered overnight or by messenger, we ask them to pay for it. It's amazing how often the other party will agree to that request—or change their mind about the urgency of the material.

7. MAKE VENDORS COMPETE FOR YOUR BUSINESS.

If you're buying a car, you shop around for the best price. Yet many people aren't as prudent when they're making purchases for the company. They get comfortable dealing with the same vendors year after year. To them, the vendor's annual 10 percent increase in the cost of certain goods and services is the price they pay for dealing with a friendly, familiar face. They never stop to think that maybe a new supplier has appeared on the scene who is willing to undercut their so-called friend to win their account.

To combat that corporate inertia, we now require three competitive bids on any purchase order over $500. That simple procedure has totally reoriented our long-term supplier relationships. In the majority of cases, we are still buying from the same vendors—but at a considerably more attractive price. It turns out that we didn't have to abandon our suppliers. Rather, we learned how eager they were to keep doing business with us.

• • •
THE MCCORMACK RULES

- At a certain point in the growth of any company, the boss can't personally keep track of every expense. But your people can't be sure of that.

- Downsizing is not an area where many entrepreneurs distinguish themselves. They cut too little or too late. They cut muscle, not fat. They resist cutting their "sacred cows." In many cases, they're incapable of making cuts at all.

- In any vibrant company, you have to be downsizing and upsizing at the same time.

- With a little imagination, every expense can be reduced.

- Whenever I see a bill with more zeroes than numbers—whether it's $500 or $50,000—I question it.

- In my experience, at least 80 percent of what a company does in a downsizing mode is what it should have done anyway.

CHAPTER 8

Assessing and Rewarding People Fairly

THE FALLACY OF THE BIGGER PAYCHECK

I was once invited to speak to the sales division of a West Coast insurance company. I was warned that I would be addressing a company in crisis. My audience consisted of 800 sales managers and salespeople. Apparently, a rift had developed between the managers and the salespeople, in large part because many salespeople, working on commissions, earned more than their bosses. As a result, the salespeople didn't respect the sales managers. The lament was familiar: "If you're so smart, why am I earning more than you?" The sales force was veering out of control.

The insurance company thought that, as an agent who has dealt with young, headstrong athletes who earn millions of dollars a year, I might have some insights for the sales force that could make them toe the line and perhaps end the conflict.

Frankly, I was puzzled that the problem even came up. There are countless situations in business and life where there is a disparity in income between two people. Yet that disparity doesn't fracture the relationship or force the lower-earning individual to cede authority and control to his richer counterpart.

That's like saying if you earn $2 million a year and come down with pneumonia, why would you listen to a doctor who's making $200,000 a year? The simple answer: The doctor knows more about pneumonia than you do—and he can help you.

This dynamic of poor manager versus rich star occurs a lot in professional life.

The editor of a daily newspaper may earn a fraction of what his star syndicated columnist rakes in. But that disparity doesn't disrupt the chain of command. It's the editor who hands out the assignments and decides what stories run on the front page and what gets buried inside. If the star columnist wants to remain a star, he listens to his editor.

Likewise with the director of a motion picture who earns considerably less than his two leading stars. Despite the smaller paycheck, a talented director will always call the shots—and have his stars believing that it's in their best interest to obey him.

I'm sure there are insurance brokers who earn more than the CEO of an insurance company, car dealers who earn more than the chairman of a car company, evening news anchors who earn more than the president of their network. But the fatter paycheck doesn't necessarily adorn them with greater knowledge or authority. That's the fallacy of the paycheck—that the size of your paycheck is somehow directly proportional to your power and standing in an organization. In many cases, it isn't.

In our organization, I cannot remember a situation where an athlete earning $5 million a year took his newfound wealth as a license to disrespect the executive at our company who was guiding his or her career and handling his or her business affairs. Both athlete and agent realize that each of them has a specific talent, that they need each other, and that they will both be better off if each of them has the freedom to do what they do best.

Actually, if the income disparity between manager and star (or employer and employee) causes a problem, the resentment usually goes the other way. The manager resents his rich client, especially if the manager feels that he is smarter and the client doesn't appreciate how much he is contributing to the client's fortune. Again, it's a familiar lament: "Who is this nineteen-year-old brat making $5 million a year from a clothing contract that I got for him!"

As the CEO of an organization with many agents and many star clients (where, mercifully, this problem doesn't come up too often), I try to temper any signs of resentment by pointing out the temporal nature of a young athlete's earning power. A professional football player stays in the NFL an average of 3.7 years. A tennis phenom can burn out or fall off the pro tour due to injuries before he or she turns twenty-one. It's no different for basketball players, skiers, figure skaters, and track stars. They only have a few years to make their mark and their millions. After that, they're finished. The manager, on the other hand, might be wiser and more experienced. The manager can be tripling his income with new clients, whereas the athlete must start a new career.

In my speech, I had very little to say to the salespeople. If they were earning big commissions, they were doing their job—which was to sell.

I turned most of my attention to the company's senior management and sales managers—because I thought they, not the salespeople, were the root of the problem. Their resentment of the hard-charging sales force fostered the conflict at the company.

I reminded the group of the temporal nature of earning power, that inevitably the industry would hit a slump, the sales force wouldn't be writing policies as fast, and the pendulum of authority would swing back to the managers.

But before that happened, it was the managers' job to convince their people that they had to work together as a team, that each of them had a job to do, and that in the long run they would all be rewarded if they accepted their roles.

The most appropriate sports analogy in this case is the relationship between the coach and players of a professional basketball team. An NBA coach on average earns about as much as the ninth man on his twelve-man roster. His salary is just a fraction of what his top six players take home. And it's public knowledge. On top of that, the players themselves have some of the most formidable egos in sports. That's not surprising since each has been the star on his team since junior high school. Each has been showered with adulation for years.

The coach must take this random assortment of high-priced, high-ego talent and mold it into a cohesive team. How does he do that?

For one thing, he reminds them how fleeting their athletic talent really is. As a team they have three, four, maybe five years together when their individual abilities are at their peak and they can mesh into a championship team. He reminds them that very few NBA teams repeat as champions precisely because it's so difficult to maintain that winning chemistry for a long period of time. The team has a brief window of opportunity to make their mark. The coaches who can make their players accept this fact never have to worry about the paycheck gap between them and their superstars. None of them is playing for merely a paycheck anymore. They're playing to win.

THE CASE AGAINST COMMISSIONS

I had the good fortune of making a nice income relatively early in my career, so I'm not uncomfortable when some of our younger executives enter the more generous realms of our compensation structure.

I don't let age affect salary decisions. If a talented and highly motivated twenty-seven-year-old is outperforming someone in his forties, the younger executive deserves to be paid more. I don't begrudge people their success because of their youth.

I don't pay women less than men because they are women.

I don't pay a married executive more than a single employee simply because the married executive has a family to support or a mortgage to maintain.

I like to think that our company has eliminated most conventional prejudices that affect employees' compensation.

However, I do have one bias. I don't like paying sales-people on a commission basis.

Theoretically, pay for play should work. Linking people's paycheck directly to productivity is the fairest way of rewarding and motivating them. But in my experience, human nature and organizational dynamics nearly always defeat this policy.

Here are three compensation scenarios that every entrepreneur will face as his sales force grows—and my reasons to avoid them.

1. NEVER COMMISSION GROSS REVENUES.

Perhaps the most insidious commission arrangement is when a sales manager or division head seeks a percentage of his group's gross sales.

The problem with this arrangement is that it instills all the wrong motivations for someone to sell.

First of all, it creates an atmosphere where all the group head cares about is gross sales rather than profitability. Given the choice between closing a million-dollar sale with a 10 percent profit margin and a $500,000 transaction at a 25 percent margin, guess which deal he would go for—even though the latter is better for the company?

Second, it invariably increases expenses. The group head will spend anything to generate more gross sales. Suddenly, he needs more salespeople. He needs to increase public awareness via advertising and promotion. He needs a major bump in his travel and entertainment budget. He has to hire consultants to create a fancier brochure or produce a sales video or construct a new sales booth for conventions.

Third, it can be internally divisive. In the desperate effort to increase sales, many managers try to increase the number of people reporting to them, often by recruiting people from other divisions. It's a nifty way to avoid increased personnel costs—after all, you're not hiring new people, merely reassigning them—but this rarely sits well with the other group heads.

2. NEVER COMMISSION NET PROFITS.

Letting a sales manager commission net profits rather than gross income is not much of an improvement. It creates a different set of problems.

For example, in our company, most of the good projects we have done commercially happen because we have taken a risk and were willing to lose money in the first year or two. If we create a sports event, we might lose $400,000 in Year One, $100,000 in Year Two, and turn a profit in Year Three. But we're willing to do that. Experience has taught us that, if we do our job well, the payoff is down the road. That's how a company grows.

But the costs of growth are in direct conflict with a manager commissioning net profits. We tried this arrangement years ago with the head of a foreign office. The net result was that he refused to take any kind of a risk—because anything that lost money in Year One was going to cost him money that year.

It turned out that we were getting all the wrong direction from his office. What we wanted was someone telling us, "We should take on this equestrian event in Germany. It will lose money the first two years, but five years later we will have tripled our investment." Instead, all he wanted to do was benefit from either the occasional one-shot quick-hit opportunity or the mature (and already profitable) ventures that we had developed. Again, the arrangement gave the executive all the wrong motivations.

3. PAY SATELLITE OFFICES WELL, BUT NOT DIFFERENTLY.

Another dangerous situation: the manager of a satellite office who wants a percentage of the business generated in his territory or by his people.

The trouble with territorial arrangements is that they transform normally rational businesspeople into territorial animals. They become reluctant to bring "outsiders" from other parts of the company into their deals—even when they know these outside experts could enhance their credibility or improve their bargaining position—because they're afraid their office would not get 100 percent credit for the transaction.

I call this the "Lone Arranger" syndrome. It afflicts anyone who insists on working alone, who perceives every triumph as an individual rather than a corporate achievement. But it is particularly virulent with branch managers who end up running all over the place trying to do deals by themselves with companies where their colleagues may already have strong relationships. The end result is that they don't get as far as quickly as they would have if they had brought the appropriate colleague into the mix. Everyone loses, especially the company, all because one manager was afraid of diluting his office's profits.

MAKE SURE YOU GET CREDIT FOR YOUR COMPANY'S PERKS

I once knew the head of a sports federation who liked to boast about how he never received any money for the work he did. Every time I'd see him he'd point out that he was volunteering his services, that his stewardship was a noble calling, and that he certainly wasn't being enriched by it.

Yet this gentleman regularly flew the world on the Concorde or, at worst, first-class. He stayed in the finest suites at luxury hotels, entertained at Michelin three-star restaurants, hosted the world's royalty at the best seats at his sport's major events, and was in turn hosted by others in the best seats at their events.

He actually had himself convinced that he wasn't getting anything from this.

Of course, what he got was a lifestyle that for a normal human being would have cost $400,000 a year. Considering that he would have to work for that income, pay taxes on it, and then shell out the cash to support the lifestyle, he was a very lucky fellow—and he should have stopped congratulating himself for his voluntarism.

I mention this because I think that a lot of owners and managers, when they discuss compensation with their employees, forget to factor in the various perks and privileges that make working at their company enjoyable.

A company's perks come in all shapes and sizes, of course. I'm not talking about the obvious ones, such as a company car or a financial management program or paid-up insurance premiums or even country club memberships, all of which have a clearly defined monetary value and are rarely overlooked in an executive's compensation package.

But what about perks such as flying business-class, use of the corporate villa in Portugal, access to season tickets on the fifty-yard line at Giants Stadium, or even keeping frequent-flyer mileage? All of these are paid for by the company and benefit no one else but the employees.

Unfortunately, most of these tend to be forgotten by boss and employee at salary reviews. The employee, for his part, will conveniently ignore the tickets to the U.S. Open, the first-class trips, and the 215,000 frequent-flyer miles he has racked up (which paid for two family vacations) when thinking about his compensation. And the company is usually not sophisticated enough to identify these perks or calculate their worth.

My point is that with the cost of business travel and entertainment nearly doubling in the last decade, companies can no longer afford to ignore the hidden value of perks and privileges. The company pays for them. The employees enjoy them. The company should get credit for them.

As a boss, you may never be able to recapture all of your employees' frequent-flyer mileage (it's virtually impossible at companies with thirty or more employees), but isn't it a good idea at least to mention the value of these miles in a salary

review? You may never be able to persuade your senior executives to sacrifice their upper-class travel style (at least not
without damaging morale), but shouldn't there be a reminder
of your generosity in their compensation?

This isn't very hard to track at most companies. All you
need is a file of the perks and privileges the company metes out
during the course of the year. If an employee is being honest with
himself about his compensation, he'll keep that file. If the company is being smart about compensation, it will keep that file, too.

DEFUSING THE BOOBY TRAPS IN YOUR ANNUAL REVIEWS

At some point during the fiscal year, a manager's mind turns
to employee reviews—the necessary and not always pleasant
task of grading your people's performance, adjusting their
compensation accordingly, and establishing their goals for
the coming year.

It's not as easy as it sounds. The route to an honest and
fair evaluation of an employee is loaded with booby traps and
fallacies. Some are devised by employees, others are built into
the system. As a manager, I know this first-hand—because
I've fallen for many of these traps myself. Here are three to
watch out for as the new year approaches.

1. RIGHT PERSON, WRONG STANDARDS.

Not every employee can measure up to company standards in
a performance appraisal. But that doesn't necessarily mean

the employee is doing a bad job. Sometimes the standards are wrong.

The following, I'm happy to report, did *not* happen at our company.

A few years back, the president of a large financial firm took it upon himself to discipline the manager of one of the firm's most profitable satellite offices at his year-end review. The president froze the manager's salary and eliminated his bonus, knowing full well that such a review would lead to the manager's resignation.

The president had his reasons. He thought the manager was an undisciplined wild card. He was never in his office, he was always late submitting his monthly sales reports, and, twice during the year, he passed up the quarterly meetings at the New York headquarters in order to help a salesperson deal with a disgruntled customer. In the president's eyes, he was not only a bad manager but unmanageable.

As expected, the manager quit. What the firm didn't expect was that his entire office would quit with him. A money-making office turned into a loser and closed within six months. The qualities that made this manager a failure by company standards—always in the "field" selling, never in his office; caring more about his people than paperwork; passing up meetings with his superiors to help a subordinate in need—made him a hero to his staff.

I can see how this happens. If everyone at your company hands their budgets in on time or wears dark suits and white shirts or puts in seventy-hour weeks, it's easy to see how the one maverick executive who doesn't follow the party line might be perceived as somehow not measuring up to company standards.

When good people don't play by your rules, perhaps you should reexamine the rules before penalizing them for a technical foul.

2. BEWARE THE TWO-MINUTE DRILL.

Some employees tend to be at their most productive in the last three months of the year—just before their scheduled performance review. I don't know if they plan it this way or if they realize they're falling short of their objectives and get desperate. But I do know that a lot of bosses improperly reward this last-minute hustle.

This is the corporate equivalent of football's two-minute drill: With time running out, the quarterback marches his hurry-up offense down the field for a last-second score. In football, it's dramatic, exciting, and sometimes even leads to victory. But in business, it's no way to lead your team.

A fair manager always endeavors to evaluate an employee's entire year, not just the most recent evidence. Before you pat someone on the back for finally closing a sale in the fourth quarter, you might want to ask what they were doing the first nine months of the year. The converse of this is also true. If someone has performed admirably during the first nine months of the year, don't punish them for falling into a bit of a slump at year's end.

3. OVERTIME OR "FACE TIME"?

"Face time" is the current phrase to describe the extra hours an employee spends at work not necessarily working but just showing his or her face. It's the employee who shows up at seven o'clock every morning and spends the next two hours ordering his breakfast, reading the newspaper, and calling his friends. Or it's the employee who never leaves before 7:30 in the evening but spends the last hours of each day with his feet up in someone else's office or on the phone arranging that evening's social schedule.

To maintain discipline and avoid internal chaos, every organization needs its own definition of "normal business hours." In most office situations, you expect people to be in by 9 A.M. and to stay until 5:00 or 5:30 P.M. A good manager states this clearly to all his employees the first day they come to work.

An employee who abuses these hours, by chronically coming in late or leaving early, shouldn't be surprised if that's reflected in his or her evaluation and compensation.

But I don't think the converse is necessarily true. Long hours are not always praiseworthy.

Unless you are a boss at a high-powered investment bank or law firm—where fourteen-hour days seem to be part of the corporate culture and are a litmus test for future partners—you should expect your people to work only long enough to get the job done.

Judge their performance, not their time sheet.

As a general rule, boasting about the hours they keep is the last resort of employees who are falling short on results. Good managers know the difference between overtime and "face time"—and they don't reward the latter.

HOW TO PUT MORE PUNCH INTO YOUR PERFORMANCE REVIEWS

I believe most managers don't enjoy the experience of a performance review because the review is, at heart, a confrontation. As the employee argues his case, struggling to put a positive spin on his performance during the previous twelve months, the manager must point out, in chapter and verse, where the employee is right and wrong. A dialogue that, in theory, should improve the employee-manager relationship quite often ends up damaging it.

Perhaps that's one reason why job reviews at many companies have turned into such predictable and bloodless routines. We all know the drill. Boss pulls employee's file. Boss scans MBO (Management by Objective) memo. Boss asks employee to comment. Employee (who wrote said memo the year before) cites achievements. They shake hands, agree on new MBO, review salary, and repeat the process the following year.

This is hardly a major "bonding" experience for either party, yet it probably has a greater impact on the employee's happiness and the company's well-being than any other discussion that year. (If you don't believe me, just think how much time you've spent rethinking the most recent job review with your boss.)

What can managers do to transform the standard review from a dispiriting affair into an enlightening one? For starters, they can ask more provocative questions. They can push for answers that reveal what's really on their employees' minds. Here are six questions that your subordinates (a) probably don't expect to hear from you but (b) would definitely like the opportunity to comment on.

1. Who are your most valuable peers or subordinates? And what can we do to make them better and make sure they stay? This is the best sort of intelligence for a boss who has long-term goals and wants to build a team that will endure. I can't think of a better way to identify the "lifers" at your company as opposed to those who are "just passing through."

2. What scares you the most about our competition? Subordinates often have a less arrogant, more respectful attitude toward competitors than their bosses do. Unlike bosses, whose egos are usually involved in the comparison, subordinates don't necessarily regard the competition's strength as a sign of their own weakness. As a manager, you might be surprised to learn where the competition is beating you.

3. Why does this company need you? The point of interest here is how drastically the employee's opinion differs from your own.

4. What did you allow to fall through the cracks during the past twelve months? Assuming you grant the employee amnesty, this question works like truth serum—a great way to discover the chinks in your organization's armor.

5. How are the company's objectives at odds with your personal goals? Is the company growing too fast, getting too big, introducing too many unfamiliar faces, losing its feeling of "family," expecting more hours than the employee is willing to give? Letting the employee express his view of any conflicts is valuable, but you'll create even more problems if you promise to

resolve these conflicts in the near future when you know you can't. That promise might allow you to gracefully ease out of this dialogue, but failing to deliver on it will set your relationship with the subordinate further back than when you started talking.

6. What are the half dozen or so areas in the coming year where you expect my unqualified support? This is the final question. Even the most closed-mouthed employees have ideas about what you can be doing for them. If an employee has been coy or unresponsive up to this point, this question will usually get him to open up—because it turns the discussion onto you.

• • •
THE McCORMACK RULES

- The trouble with territorial arrangements is that they transform normally rational businesspeople into territorial animals.

- When good people don't play by your rules, perhaps you should reexamine the rules before penalizing them for a technical foul.

- A fair manager evaluates an employee's entire year, not just the most recent evidence.

- A good manager knows the difference between overtime and "face time"—and he doesn't reward the latter.

Advanced Techniques

THE SIGNS OF A BUTTONED-UP COMPANY

Not long ago one of our salespeople set up a meeting with a large manufacturer on the West Coast. When he called the company's headquarters a few days before the meeting to get directions from the airport, an assistant told him, "Don't worry about that. We're sending our helicopter to pick you up."

When I heard about this, I was impressed. It's not every day our people receive such royal treatment. My first impression was: "The company must be doing really well." But then a more troubling thought entered my mind. What kind of company sends an $800-an-hour helicopter to pick up one of our salespeople? If it were a customer, I could understand it. The courtesy might help close a sale. But our man was a seller, not a buyer. We were asking them for money.

I found this sort of excess disturbing and made a mental note that the company might not be as sound as it appeared to be. A few weeks later I read in the paper that the company had posted a huge quarterly loss and the board of directors had sacked the CEO, in large part because of runaway spending.

I'm not making any claim for being clairvoyant or implying that the helicopter caused all the red ink at the company. But to any moderately alert person, the helicopter was certainly a symbol that all was not right at the company, that it was not as buttoned-up and cost-efficient as it should be.

I think all organizations give off little clues about their efficiency or lack thereof. If you're alert to the clues, you can pick up valuable early-warning signals about whether doing business with that company will be a happy or sad experience. Here is a highly idiosyncratic list of clues—which all of us are exposed to every day—that have helped me form some valuable impressions.

1. OVERNIGHT DELIVERY.

I always think twice about a company where employees send any and every package via overnight mail, even when it's not urgent. I wonder what other excesses are going on there.

Conversely, if I asked someone at another company to send me a package via overnight mail, I'd be impressed if they hesitated and then asked me to give them my courier account number. In other words, I'll get the package the next day, but I'm going to pay for it. That tells me that company is buttoned-up. They're cheap but smart.

2. PHONE RINGS.

I was once given a tour of the telemarketing operations of a very profitable bank in Delaware. On the wall was a huge sign congratulating the employees for answering 99.2 percent of all incoming calls the previous month within two rings—a company record.

There is no quicker way to gauge a company's efficiency than by counting how many rings it takes for your call to get through.

As I say, this bank was extremely profitable.

3. THE PARKING LOT.

I learned something good about that bank in Delaware before I ever entered their building. The clue was in their parking policy: Senior bank executives were intentionally assigned the worst parking spaces in the enormous lot, farthest from the office door. Junior employees had the best spaces. This flip-flop of traditional executive privilege was corny but had a loftier purpose: It forced senior management to ride the parking lot shuttle bus each day and mingle with a multitude of employees.

That was another clue that I was dealing with an extraordinary organization.

4. PHONE MAIL.

A lot of people regard phone mail as a sign of efficiency. But I don't. I would rather have immediate contact with a human. To me phone mail is a sign of a company that's losing touch with customers and getting too cute with high technology. I realize I may be in the minority on this, but it's a symbol of machines superseding people. We have phone mail in some parts of our company, but I think it's an evil technology. When I get imprisoned in the phone mail environment and have to cut through all the recordings and messages to reach a human being, I often lose interest in the company.

5. RESPONSE TIME.

I'm also quick to judge a company and its people by how quickly they respond to one of my letters or if they don't respond at all. Response time is a telling clue.

I'm continually amazed by people who never bother to respond to my letters. I realize they have their reasons. They might be uncomfortable saying no to my proposal, or they don't want to offend me, or they're not interested. But there's no excuse for not acknowledging that you have received the letter. You can write:

- Thank you for your letter, but we're not interested.

- I referred it to Mr. Smith.

- I'll get back to you in three weeks.

- It isn't appropriate at the present time.

- Let's discuss.

- Next time you're in town, can we meet?

This is just a partial menu of stock responses. Yet a lot of people neglect to employ them in a routine letter that takes seconds to fire off. That tells me something about how they do business, and it's not necessarily good.

These five random examples of how managers deal with seemingly mundane matters—and how else can you describe overnight mail, employee parking, ringing telephones, voice mail, and unsolicited mail?—are actually examples of very advanced management techniques. They are evidence of managers coming up with ingenious and disciplined solutions to problems that many of us overlook or take for granted every day. In my mind, that makes them advanced techniques because they demonstrate a mastery of managing people, money, and work.

Run Your Company the Same Way You Spend Your Spare Cash

I was once interviewed by a personal finance magazine to find out how "civilians" like me (as opposed to investment professionals) invest their money. I came up with with what I thought were some snappy sound bites and rules for investors. But when the article appeared, I realized that my "investment philosophy," such as it was, bore a remarkable resemblance to my management style—and that my rules for spending my spare cash applied to anyone running a growing business.

1. Bet on the Jockey, not the Horse.

In my line of work, I get to meet with the heads of a lot of public companies. If I'm impressed with the CEO of a company, I'll buy stock in his company—even if I don't really understand his business. This "bet on the jockey" approach has paid off more often that it has burned me. I don't know anything about oil refining or selling soap or insuring high-risk but I've bet my money on those types of companies after I've met their CEOs. First-rate management tends to deliver first-rate results.

It's the same within our company. There have been many occasions when I've plucked talented people out of their comfortable niches and given them assignments that, on the surface, didn't conform with their education or expertise. My thinking: If they have talent, they can manage anything. If the profit potential is there, they'll find a way to tap it.

2. Pick up the Discards.

I've always been attracted to companies that have fallen out of favor because of bad news—the stocks that panicky investors discount or discard. Chaos creates opportunities and bargains if you can keep your eye on the fundamentals. That's why I bought Texaco after it lost a $4 billion lawsuit to Pennzoil and Johnson & Johnson after the Tylenol tampering scare. I just couldn't see Texaco disappearing from the scene. (I'm not infallible. I also bought Pan Am shares at what I thought was rock-bottom, but the airline crash-landed into bankruptcy.)

As a management principle, this approach works in hiring talented people. If I hear that one of our competitors is in trouble, I'm not shy about skimming off the cream of their executive crop. Some of our best people are happy and grateful refugees from chaotic situations.

It also applies if you're acquiring businesses. If you know a rival company is on its way down, you can often pick up its most valuable pieces at distress sale prices.

3. THINK LONG TERM.

It's not unusual for me to hold on to a stock for two decades or more. I don't worry about occasional hiccups in quarterly earnings or temporary dips in the share price. I'm more interested in where the company will be three, five, or ten years down the road. If I'm comfortable with top management, that patience is usually rewarded.

I try to apply that same patience in venturing into new areas at our company. If we start a tennis tournament from scratch, we know that we'll lose money in Year One and maybe break even in Year Two. But I'm not worried about the red ink at the start. I'm looking at Years Four, Five, and beyond. If we do our job, as the event gains acceptance by the top players and, in turn, becomes more interesting to the ticket-buying public, the profits will come—and continue growing.

4. INVEST IN WHAT YOU KNOW.

If I were a computer wizard, I'd probably invest in high-tech stocks. If I were a banker, I'd invest in banks. But I don't know those industries—and don't pretend to. So I don't invest in them (unless Rule 1 is in force). For better or worse, sports is what I know. So sports and leisure companies make up a large part of my portfolio. If I don't know the industry or management personally, I rely on other investment pros for diversification (*i.e.*, mutual funds).

Two management principles stem from this rule. First, sticking with what you know forces you to admit what you don't know. For example, I know nothing about computers or high technology. Except for cellular phones and electric razors, I'm not obsessed with gadgets. But I realize our company needs to invest in high-tech equipment to grow.

Which leads to the second principle: If you don't know something, turn it over to people who do know. I have no idea what our in-house computer experts do, but I trust them to invest our resources wisely. If I've invested wisely in the people who know what they're doing, that's all I need to know.

5. A KNOWN RISK ISN'T RISKY.

All investments are risky. Admitting that to yourself is the first step in reducing the risk.

I was considering an investment in an insurance company some years ago, largely because I knew and admired the CEO. I asked him once what the biggest risks in his business were. He said, "There are lots of risks. Our policy holders can suddenly get accident prone, driving up our costs. State regulators can put a limit on the premiums we can charge, driving down our profit margins. Competitors can start a price war. But, you know, Mark, these so-called risks aren't really risky to me—because we're aware of them and we have contingency plans to deal with them. The biggest risk is the one you can't name, the disaster lurking out there that you wouldn't imagine in your wildest dreams."

That struck me as an enlightened view about risk. Thinking that you have all the answers is actually riskier than knowing that you don't.

As a manager I've tried to apply that outlook on risk whenever I have to decide whether to invest in a new project. I'd much rather put my money behind someone who, despite doing all the homework, can admit that the concept is risky. At least I know that person is a realist who appreciates how even the best-laid plans can fail. People who want my support because their concept is a "sure thing" don't understand risk—and have a lot more homework to do.

THE LEADER BOARD
ALWAYS CHANGES

Many people think that a manager is never more a pure manager than when he is controlling a crisis. I can see why people believe that. There's something grand and dramatic about an executive calmly facing down doom and heroically marshaling the troops to overcome disaster.

I'm not sure I buy that. I put a lot more value on a manager who can see a crisis coming months or years in advance—and knows how to marshal the troops so the crisis never gets a chance to happen. As the saying goes, an ounce of prevention is worth a pound of cure. We should exalt the people who prevent problems even more than we admire the people who cure them.

We should also exalt managers who can create a sense of crisis even when a crisis doesn't exist.

There's a dangerous tendency at any company to get complacent when things are going well. People take success for granted. Even worse, they adamantly oppose any sort of change. "If it ain't broke, don't fix it," is their motto.

I also don't buy that. I've learned over the years that no matter how great things may be going now, everything changes three or four years out. You can bet on it. And you can't afford to stand still. In today's climate of fickle tastes and accelerated change, a more appropriate management motto might be: "If it ain't broke, break it."

Obvious as this point may seem to some, I can see how a lot of people miss it. There's a certain comfort in looking at your current business and projecting it out five or ten years in a smooth line of modest but steady growth. If you're selling $1 million of widgets now, it's not unreasonable to expect to double that in a few years. Unfortunately, this fallacy-laden thinking ignores the possibility that a competitor will (a) build a better widget (reducing demand for your widget) or (b) lower the price (eroding your profit margins) or (c) create a product that replaces widgets (eliminating your widget business altogether). The moment you draw that uninterrupted line of steady growth, you can be sure there's someone out there thinking of ways to erase it or take it from you.

The sports business, I suspect, has made it easier for me to appreciate this. No business is more changeable or unpredictable than sports, where champions can turn into also-rans overnight. Yet I constantly have to remind our people that change is constant and prod them away from the fallacious thinking that leads to complacency. Here are three fallacies that often blind people to an impending crisis.

1. THE LEADER BOARD NEVER CHANGES.

When things are going great, people find it difficult to imagine a time when things won't be as great. They think that their current success will never end, or that they can repeat it forever. It's precisely at those moments that I like to remind people that the leader board always changes.

For example, four years ago, the top four golfers in the world according to the Sony Ranking were Nick Faldo, Greg Norman, Nick Price, and Bernhard Langer. We represented all four of them. It would have been nice to let the people in our golf division bask in that happy circumstance or delude themselves that it would continue forever. But things change. Today, we only manage two of the four top golfers. That's why I'm constantly reminding our people that we can't afford to think we own the leader board. And we have to run our business as if the leader board can change overnight—because it will.

If you think your people are victims of this sort of complacency, here's a worthwhile exercise to combat this fallacy: Go back five or ten years in your company and review who your top competitors were, who the leaders were in market share, even who the top performers within the company were. Chances are the leaders back then were considerably different from the leaders today. What makes you think things will be any different ten years hence?

2. A JOB WELL DONE GOES WELL REWARDED.

Another fallacy centers on the curious notion that if you do a job exceptionally well for other people, those same people will be glad to pay you to continue doing that job forever. Not true. At some point, I've learned, they begin to think they can do your job themselves.

One of our company's great advantages is our international connections. We have seventy-three offices in twenty-eight countries. Most domestic organizations in sports—whether they're teams or leagues or federations—don't have that international reach. As a result, a sports league might hire us to sell the broadcast rights to its games around the world. They don't know how to get their games on television in parts of Europe or the Far East. We do. So we start out with a modest sale to a foreign network. After a year or two, as public interest builds and the television audience grows, the rights fees grow as well. Not surprisingly, our fees grow, too. If we continue to do our job well, in seven or eight years it's quite possible that we have helped our client build a substantial business. You'd think the client would be grateful that we took his international broadcast revenues from zero to millions—and want us on the payroll forever.

It doesn't always work out that way. There comes a moment when the client starts to focus less on the money he's making and more on the fee we are commissioning for our efforts. Ironically, this tends to happen when the revenues reach a critical mass that the client never imagined and you would normally expect everyone to be at their happiest. At that point, the client thinks he might take the international sales job in-house by hiring someone at a fraction of our fee. Why not? The client has walked through all the doors we've opened. He's seen how we price the product and draft the contract. How smart do you have to be to renew a contract for three years? And why do we need McCormack?

I've seen this happen often enough to know it's true. You build a mousetrap for people and eventually they think they can catch mice themselves. Internally, of course, our people don't always catch this irony. They think doing excellent work will be excellently rewarded. They're so pleased with the increased revenues they're bringing in, they forget that the client sometimes underestimates how hard we are working and is more inclined to say "What have you done for me lately?" than "Thank you."

That's why I'm constantly reminding our people to talk to the client and to add elements to the relationship that he can't live without. Doing a good job is no protection. And doing a great job can actually create a crisis.

3. THE MYTH OF THE "COMFORTABLE LEAD."

Perhaps the most dangerous fallacy is the one that says you can relax because you have lapped the field. Let's say your company has a 40 percent market share in your industry or territory and your nearest rival has 10 percent. It's human nature for your people to feel self-satisfied with that competitive edge and to regard with disdain each new upstart who dares to challenge your lead. But people forget that it only takes three or four of these little gnat-like competitors, each assaulting your business on different flanks, to distract you, to chip away at your market share, and to slow down or reverse your momentum. You ignore these upstarts at your peril.

I suppose any manager could drive the point home by pointing to IBM or Sears or the American steel industry, all of whom were seriously undone by a host of gnat-like competitors that grew at their expense. But I prefer to tell the story of Hobart Manley, who was one of the leading amateur golf players in the U.S. and a student of Byron Nelson. Manley was playing in the U.S. Amateur championships in Minnesota, paired up against a local fifteen-year-old boy who had qualified for the tournament and was being followed around by his parents and neighbors. Manley got up four strokes early in the round against the boy, when suddenly the boy started crying in full view of his parents and supporters. Manley thought, "I'm killing this kid in front of his family," and started to feel sorry for him. Suddenly, he started playing poorly and ended up losing the match to the youngster.

The next time he saw his teacher, Byron Nelson, Manley told him what had happened. Nelson (a gentleman but also a fierce competitor who once won eleven PGA tournaments in a row) replied, "That's exactly where you want them—crying! And when you get them there, you want to put your heel on top of them and grind them into the dust."

That may sound harsh, but it's reality. There is no such thing as a comfortable lead. Managers who cannot maintain a sense of impending crisis within their organization will probably be facing real crises sooner than they imagine.

How to Open a European Office

The smartest thing our company has ever done was to go international as soon as we could. We realized that America's insa-
tiable appetite for sports was exportable, especially in our core
sports of golf and tennis which, unlike quintessentially American
sports such as baseball or football, were played in every corner
of the globe. We had an established market of interest for our
golfers and tennis players. We didn't have to educate companies and executives in Great Britain, Japan, Australia, South
America, and Western Europe about these sports.

But building an international network was hardly a piece
of cake. Opening up a foreign office is not just a matter of
renting office space, hanging up a shingle, and saying, "We're
open for business." It is one of the trickiest management tasks
an entrepreneur will ever face—and over the years I've
watched dozens of American companies, including all of our
company's competitors, fail at it.

If you're considering taking your business abroad (and
you should), the following lessons, learned slowly and sometimes painfully by us, will spare you considerable heartache
and losses.

1. Hire a Salesperson.

The most important decision you make—whether you're opening an office in London, Paris, Tokyo, Stockholm, Milan, or
anywhere—is your first employee. He or she will drive the

office. If you get that decision wrong, you won't get a chance to hire a second employee.

No matter what business you're in, the first employee should be a salesperson. You need the office to pay for itself as quickly as possible, so you need sales and cash flow. Without cash flow, you don't have a foreign office; you only have a foreign address.

2. HIRE NATIONALS.

The temptation at many companies is to take the Ugly American route—that is, pluck up a perfectly competent American employee and drop him in a foreign land and say, "Develop it."

We never did that. We have always hired nationals to run our offices. Britons run our London offices, a Swede runs our Stockholm office, a Frenchman runs our Paris office, a Hungarian runs our Budapest office, and so on. The theory is simple: It's easier to train a Swedish or French national about our methods and philosophy than it is to train one of our American employees about how to do business in Sweden or France. The American doesn't know the language or culture as well as the national. He doesn't have the contacts. He doesn't know the ins and outs of that country's sports. He has no history or background or professional standing. He has to build his reputation from scratch.

I realize that there's a certain comfort level in hiring Americans overseas if you're an American company. They walk, talk, dress, and think like you. You're comfortable with them. But that's the most pernicious and narrow-minded kind of prejudice. And I urge every company to resist it. Injecting some foreign talent into your company can give you a whole new way of looking at your company's problems. You can't call yourself an international company if you don't have a lot of international accents running through it.

3. PROVIDE BACKUP—BUT RENT IT, DON'T BUY IT.

Once you've hired a national who can sell, you have to provide that person with some administrative and financial support in the form of accountants, bookkeepers, and lawyers.

Our experience in opening up our various offices on the Continent has taught us that you will need this support fairly early on. A salesperson by definition is interested in sales and is not too concerned about contracts, legal issues, and accounting matters. So you have to supply him with excellent backup the moment he starts selling.

You don't necessarily have to hire these lawyers and accountants full-time. In fact, you're better off retaining them at the start on a project basis.

A lot of companies make the mistake of having that sales and administration capacity from day one—before they ever have their first penny of sales. I remember one of our competitors making a big splash a few years ago by opening up a foreign office with five executives (none of whom, incidentally, was native to that country). That's a lot of overhead for a venture whose success is still an open question. They never hired a sixth executive.

Ideally, your second full-time hire should be another salesperson. Then a third salesperson. By the time you have three to five people in an office, that's when you need a full-time accountant.

4. BEWARE THE FIRST HURDLE.

When we first decided to expand into Europe out of our London office—and keep in mind that, to our London office, doing business in France, Germany, and Italy was considered an "international" sale—we started by having London-based people travel to those countries and see if there was any business for us there. Our goal was to get enough business in a country to justify having someone there permanently. For example, in the mid-1970s we were generating $50,000 in revenues in Italy without having anyone there, simply by having our London people fly in occasionally. To install an Italian national in a small office in Milan would cost us $100,000 in salary and overhead.

There comes a moment in time when you have to decide if that is a step you're prepared to take. You can't do any more business in Italy unless you have a daily presence there. But opening up an Italian office means that Italy suddenly goes from a $50,000 profit to a $50,000 loss. Are you willing to absorb that loss in the hope that there will be much more profit in the years to come?

That's a classic entrepreneurial hurdle: going from a small, easy profit to a loss to a bigger profit. Fortunately, we've always considered sports and sports marketing to be a growth industry—and we've been willing to jump that hurdle.

Be aware of this hurdle as you expand overseas. There will always be a moment when you will ask yourself, "Why do I have to open up a foreign office? I can do it from here at home and make a tidy profit." How you answer that question usually determines how your company will grow.

5. AVOID JOINT VENTURES.

Setting up an overseas office via a joint venture or partnership with an established person or company in that country is another common route. But I don't recommend it.

When we first started in London and decided to expand into the rest of Europe, we had very little business on the Continent and, as I've said, hiring people and opening up offices did not make economic sense. So we appointed "representatives" in each country. We had a German advertising agency working for us, an Italian shoe manufacturer, and a French lawyer.

There are at least two problems with such joint venture arrangements.

First, if your partner understands your business, he tends to put the good opportunities into his company and the not-so-good opportunities into your joint venture. Or he treats your activities as an afterthought, turning to it on Friday afternoons from 3 P.M. to 5 P.M. after he has finished his real business for the week. So you end up with a joint venture consisting of "seconds" and "discards."

Second, if you team up with someone who doesn't understand your business but is quick and bright, you run the risk of educating them too well. While you're making money together, they are learning everything about your business. They are establishing themselves as the local authority, at your expense, and in time they may even start up their own business and compete with you.

That, more or less, is what happened to us on our first foray into Europe. Within the year, we fired all our representatives and began hiring full-time nationals who could sell.

6. SELL TO THE STEREOTYPE.

I know it's dangerous to traffic in national stereotypes, but there's some truth in them. Italians are emotional. Frenchmen are intellectually proud. Swedes are dour. Germans are precise. It's important to remember these national characteristics when you start up in Europe—because they can dramatically influence how you go about making a sale.

Let's consider, for example, the concept of selling corporate sponsorship to a sporting event. One of the main benefits of sponsorship is the hospitality element, the opportunity for a sponsoring company to invite friends, guests, and customers to the event and entertain them in a tent or marquee.

Five years ago, when we started seeking corporate sponsors for one of our tennis tournaments in Germany, we were amazed to discover that German companies were not interested in hospitality. It was a foreign concept to them.

The Germans thought that if they were being invited to an event they were being bribed. They also weren't too keen about attending a sports event during a weekday; they felt guilty about being out of the office for the day. But mostly, we concluded, it stemmed from the German character. Two German executives sitting in the same office all day will call each other Herr Schmidt and Herr Marx. If they go on holiday together, they will call each other Gunther and Rainer. When they come back to the office, they will revert back to Herr Schmidt and Herr Marx.

So the idea of hospitality and getting to know clients and customers better in a convivial atmosphere—i.e., mixing business and pleasure—was an enigma to the Germans.

Thus, a big part of selling sports sponsorship to the Germans meant educating them about how hospitality works at an event and convincing them that it had a benefit.

That's not the approach we needed in Italy. To some Italian sponsors, hospitality is a more important element than television coverage or exposure of the company logo around the site. Italians are delighted to be out of the office for a day. They put a high premium on good food and beverage and stylish surroundings. And they're very comfortable surrounding themselves with friends and professional acquaintances and conducting business in such a quasi-social environment. So when we sell sponsorship in Italy, we cannot say enough about hospitality.

And so it goes throughout Europe. Each country is different. In England, the hospitality tents are brimming with guests on Thursday and Friday, but they won't be on Saturday and Sunday—because the British are delighted to take off a business day but the weekends have been promised to their families.

In France, the hospitality venues are almost a fashion show. It's very important to see and be seen—so we design and sell the venue accordingly.

In Sweden, you do not want to make the hospitality venue too luxurious. Guests will criticize a sponsor whose tent is too nice, whose food is too good and abundant. You almost have to lower your standards to achieve the "common touch."

How to Respond When Business Goes Bad

One of the best pieces of advice I ever received taught me how to cope with an economic downturn. Our business had been expanding rapidly (perhaps a little too rapidly) at a time in the 1970s when the American economy went into a tailspin. Corporations reduced their marketing budgets, and sports marketing (as you can imagine, not always the top priority at every company) was one of the first areas where people started slashing. The cuts hit our company hard, and they hit quickly.

Our revenue projections went from being bullish to depressing. There was a strong possibility that we would have to cancel some projects and curtail our growth plans.

What cheered me up was this sage piece of wisdom from a CEO familiar with our company.

"Recessions are a necessary corrective," he said. "They weed out the weaklings. They can also be a great opportunity for you. The best organizations move forward in a recession."

Over the years, as our business has weathered several more down cycles, I've come to appreciate these words more and more. I've also learned to act on them.

The following are six strategies to follow in a recession.

1. Relearn your core business.

One of the dangers of a surging economy is that it can confuse you about what your core business really is. I've seen this happen in our organization when times are really good and we are making money in some unexpected areas. For example, if we can generate phenomenal profit margins from selling an athlete client's T-shirts at sporting events, I can see how some of our people might find the T-shirt industry very attractive. Someone might even propose that we invest in a T-shirt manufacturer. Lean times, however, are a great remedy for this delusion. Lean times will teach us to stick to what we do best. They bring us back to reality. They remind us that our core business is athlete representation, not retail or apparel.

2. INCREASE MARKET SHARE.

If you are a leader in your field, it's easier to increase your market share during lean times than when times are good. In a strong economy, there's room for everyone. New competitors jump into your industry. Ambitious employees branch out on their own, perhaps taking one or two clients with them. If you're not careful, these upstarts can chip away at your share of the business.

Recessions are the perfect time to strike back. The best companies will always do better in a tough economy than the fringe or marginal companies. They have the resources to cut prices if necessary, maintain their high-quality level, or even offer enhanced services, all of which can make life tough for their competitors.

3. INTRODUCE MUCH-NEEDED AUSTERITIES.

Good times tend to breed a taste for the good life. No matter how disciplined your organization is, when business is booming, employees often become seduced by the perquisites of

243

corporate life. For senior executives, luxuries such as first-class air travel, hotel suites, hired cars, or new office furniture become routine expenses. And this snowballs all the way down the chain of command.

Streamlining during boom times is tough. Like cutting people's salaries, it's demoralizing and hard to justify. Recessions are the best time for much-needed austerity measures—because no one in their right mind can argue with you.

4. IDENTIFY INTERNAL WEAKNESSES.

An economic downturn can also brutally expose any weak links among your personnel. The real winners at your company tend to become even more creative and more resourceful during a recession, whereas the dead weight just complains that "customers aren't spending like they used to." If you ever considered paring down your payroll, a recession will pinpoint where you should start.

5. GET DISCIPLINED ABOUT CASH FLOW.

Recessions should also inspire you to get a grip on your company's financial controls. In this case, I'm referring specifically to cash flow and receivables. In a strong economy, people often aren't as focused as they should be about getting paid on time. Everything's great. There's plenty of money floating around. They know they will get paid eventually.

If your salespeople are more interested in doing deals and think collecting the cash is beneath them, an economic downturn can be a worthwhile learning experience.

6. MAKE A BOLD MOVE.

If you can afford it, a recession can be the perfect moment for a bold strategic move—such as acquiring a company or building a new store or opening a new office or starting a new division. Not only will it stun your competition, but with the market bottoming out, you will be doing so at bargain prices.

BAD NEWS BY FAX, GOOD NEWS BY MAIL

Most managers treat bad news the same way they treat criticism. They either deny it or demean it. Rarely do they accept it or deal with it. Even more rarely do they demand it.

To prove my point, reread the first paragraph. The paragraph itself is a criticism. Now, what was your first reaction to it? Did you think it was true but didn't apply to you? (That's denying it.) Did you think it was ludicrously off the mark? (That's demeaning it.) Or did you agree with it and conjure images of how you deal with criticism? (That's accepting it.) But when was the last time you actively sought honest criticism from your colleagues or subordinates? (That's demanding it.)

It's no different with bad news, which carries with it an implied criticism that we have somehow managerially failed.

As managers, our first impulse on hearing bad news is to deny it. Part of that is a survival mechanism. I know when someone in our company relays bad news to me—disastrous ticket sales at a weekend sporting event, a client defection, a major sponsor backing out of a tournament—my instinct is to soften the blow. I go through all sorts of mental gymnastics to convince myself the news is not as bad as it sounds:

- "It's the event's first year. Ticket sales are always slow in Year One."

- "We didn't really want that client, and we still have the best client list in the business."

- "We'll find another sponsor."

That's denial (and not necessarily bad). I need it to stay motivated.

On the other hand, I've seen managers use denial to no good purpose other than to avoid dealing with bad news. I sat in on a meeting at another company recently and listened as a subordinate reported quarterly sales figures well below expectations. Rather than confront this disturbing news, the subordinate's boss let it slide without comment. I'm not sure why. Perhaps he was afraid to discuss it further because digging deeper would reveal a management lapse on his part. Perhaps he didn't want to embarrass the subordinate in a public forum. Perhaps the boss didn't realize the revenue shortfall was bad news (the ultimate denial). Whatever the reason, letting bad news go unremarked on, whether the remarks are supportive or scathing, is bad management. Whatever else you choose to do with bad news, at least acknowledge it. Anything less and your people eventually won't know the difference between good news and bad.

I think you can tell a lot about managers by how they deal with truly monstrous bad news. Do they panic or rise to the occasion? Do they think only of themselves or do they think of everyone else, too?

My rule of thumb is: The bigger the disaster, the calmer I have to be. Over the years we have pinned our manpower, cash, and reputation on projects (our adventure producing a Broadway musical, for example) that, in hindsight, were sheer folly. We didn't know that, of course. No one sets out to create a fiasco. But as the bad news came tumbling in and the losses piled up, all I could do was laugh about it. That was the only sane response.

For one thing, I didn't want our people to see me worried. People take their cues from the boss. If I'm depressed, they're even more depressed. And depressed employees rarely perform at their best.

Second, some disasters *are* comical. When everyone in the company is 100 percent wrong about a sure thing, the joke's on all of us.

Third, it helps maintain perspective. We're in business to take risks. Lives have not been lost. We're not curing cancer. Let's put it behind us and move on.

The most crucial similarity between criticism and bad news, though, is that you have to demand it to get it. And you have to demand it sooner rather than later. Bad news delayed or delivered slowly is bad news squared.

Johann Rupert, the head of the Richemont luxury group, owners of Alfred Dunhill, Cartier, Rothmans, and other brands, told me that he has a stated policy where his people must send him bad news by fax (*i.e.,* immediately) and good news by mail (*i.e.,* take your time).

Rupert says this is the best way to stop employees from running to him with every positive bulletin. If things are going according to plan (or even better), he doesn't need to know that right away. Good news doesn't require action or reaction. Bad news does.

Yet, as a manager, Rupert is shrewd enough to know that good news is the only message that his people are eager to convey to him. With bad news, they hesitate. And every hour of hesitation can be costly.

So he has constructed a policy that encourages the instant delivery of bad news. He knows that, given the choice, employees will delay or disguise bad news. Rupert's "bad news by fax, good news by mail" policy eliminates that choice.

I encourage every manager to come up with a system that does the same.

THE POWER OF THE UNANNOUNCED VISIT

Back in my school days, I was always of two minds when the teacher announced that we would have a major test the following week.

On the one hand, I appreciated the warning. It gave my classmates and me plenty of time to study and bring ourselves up to speed on the day of the exam.

Yet, it seemed to me that a "pop quiz"—the occasional unannounced exam that confronted you the moment you entered the classroom—was a far more effective way to find out if we had really "mastered" the material.

The best teachers, of course, knew this. And so they evaluated us through a combination of scheduled and unscheduled testing. They kept us on our toes, on permanent alert. We could never fall behind on our reading assignments or show up to class unprepared—because we never knew what to expect.

I think all of us as managers could learn a thing or two from the motivational strategies of teachers.

In my mind, regularly scheduled meetings (whether they take place weekly, monthly, or quarterly) are the business equivalent of the announced exam.

This isn't all bad. The upside is that planning a meeting well ahead of time lets people point toward it. It gives them a deadline. It motivates them to be buttoned-up, to tie up loose ends that otherwise may end up unraveled. All of this increases the likelihood that the meeting will achieve whatever purpose you had for calling it in the first place.

The downside, however, is that some employees attach more importance to looking good at the meeting than to actually getting things done. They are great at gearing up for the meeting—preparing reports on what they have done and excuses for what they haven't. But after the meeting disbands, they never follow up (at least, not until the next meeting is announced).

It's as if the meeting never happened. Like the student who crams for a big test and then promptly forgets all he's learned the moment the test ends, these people may score high marks with their boss, but it's no way to run a business.

That's why I'm a big believer in the corporate "pop quiz"—whether it's in the form of an unannounced meeting, a surprise visit, or a casual talk in the hall. You can learn a lot about the areas your employees are neglecting if you ask pointed questions when they are not expecting them.

There's nothing particularly insidious about this, nor am I suggesting that you use pop quizzes to terrorize employees into a constant state of red alert. Ideally, your employees shouldn't even sense that they are being tested.

Not long ago, in the course of doing a profile on our company, a national magazine wanted to set up a photograph of me and several executives in our New York conference room. We assembled a random group around the table. My job was to appear as if I was locked in a serious discussion with someone. I turned to an executive who had just returned from Eastern Europe (where we are involved in some major projects) for his impressions about the changing political climate there. It was only small talk, but I could tell by his remarks that he was on top of his subject. Because it was unrehearsed, that spontaneous two-minute exchange probably did more to reassure me about that area of the company than an elaborate two-hour meeting ever could have. The executive passed with flying colors—and he had no idea he was taking an exam.

Of course, there are more aggressive forms of this sort of spot testing—which you may need to employ when you suspect the truth may be different from what people are telling you.

Sometimes the results can be startling and dramatic.

I know one entrepreneur who virtually saved a company from bankruptcy by making an unannounced visit.

About a year ago this very successful tycoon had reacquired a European entertainment company from a holding company that had overextended itself. When he had originally sold the entertainment company several years earlier, it was a thriving enterprise—and he got top dollar for it. But on his second go-round as owner, he noticed that the company seemed to have lost its momentum. The profit margins weren't as healthy, growth had slowed down, and they seemed to be losing business opportunities to competitors they once could have ignored.

The tycoon gathered his top people in Los Angeles to review the situation and figure out how to reenergize his new property. It didn't take long for the tycoon to see that the meeting was going nowhere. None of his lieutenants had the answer.

"Well, ladies and gentlemen," he said, "why don't we find out first-hand?"

And with that they all boarded a plane to Europe and parked themselves at 7 A.M. in the lobby of the company's headquarters. The tycoon secured a list of all employees and, with his assistants' help, sat there unannounced all day, jotting down when people showed up at work and when they left. The clerical staff, it turned out, straggled in between 9:30 and 10:00, at least sixty minutes after office hours began. Many of the executives came strolling in around 11:00 and left at 4:00 in the afternoon.

The next day the tycoon dismissed half the staff. His unannounced visit had revealed what was truly wrong at the company. I doubt if he would have gotten the same results if he had announced that he was coming.

SUPERSTARS PLAY BY DIFFERENT RULES

The goal of any manager is to hire good people and help them develop into superstar achievers within the organization. But grooming superstars can easily turn into a high-class headache.

The good news is that you have top-notch performers working for you. The bad news is that, once they reach their exalted status, superstars often want to play by different rules.

You see this all the time in sports.

A champion boxer usually has a slight edge with the judges in a close bout; the challenger has to knock him out or beat him convincingly to take away his title.

In the mid-1980s, when the great Chicago Bears running back Walter Payton was near the end of his career, it seemed to me that the entire NFL treated him with reverence and awe. Players almost apologized when they tackled him.

The same with Bjorn Borg. He was a great player who never lost his temper or questioned a call on the court. I always thought that if he ever disagreed with a call, given his stature and gentlemanly reputation, he could walk up to the chair and get the call reversed.

A few years ago, a best-selling book chronicled the Chicago Bulls's 1990–1991 season. It was called *The Jordan Rules* and was really about the special treatment accorded megastar Michael Jordan by the league, coaches, referees, players, media, and team owners. I'm not sure I would have enjoyed the challenge of being Bulls coach Phil Jackson and having to walk the fine line between being Jordan's boss and clearly being dependent on him for success.

That's the mixed blessing of superstars. You love the competitive edge they give you. But the bigger they get, the tougher they are to manage and the harder you have to work to keep their peers happy.

Some managers handle their business superstars by invoking the "800-Pound Gorilla" rule (derived from the joke, "Where does an 800-pound gorilla sit? Wherever he wants.").

They treat their top performers like 800-pound gorillas and let them do virtually anything they want. If the superstar identifies a new opportunity, he doesn't have to go through the usual channels to invest his time and the company's resources in this new area. Top management doesn't hesitate to give him the green light. This approach can work as long as the superstar knows his place, but managers always risk creating a monster. At some point the gorilla gets so big, he sits on them.

Some managers take the opposite approach, with equally disastrous results. Instead of giving their superstars free rein, they ignore them or unconsciously stifle them. Management guru Peter Drucker calls this "feeding problems and starving opportunities." For years Drucker has been asking new clients to identify their top-performing people. Then he asks the clients, "What are they assigned to?" Almost without exception, says Drucker, the top performers are assigned to problems, to old businesses that are sinking faster than forecast, in the hope that these fading divisions will respond to the superstar's magic touch. Then Drucker asks, "Who takes care of the opportunities?" Invariably, the opportunities are left to fend for themselves.

I don't have an all-purpose magic formula for managing superstars. Organizations and top performers vary so widely that any generalization would be pointless. But I do know this: If you want to keep your top performer happy, give them first crack at the hot emerging areas in your business. Don't assign them to the trouble spots that have only a slim chance of coming back to life. Your superstars and your business will be better for it.

The other thorny managerial problem is what to do when your non-superstars think they deserve to play by the superstar's rules. The reality in business is this: The more you have accomplished, the more leeway you have to do what you want to do. It's interesting how often people misjudge or overestimate their achievements and use it as a license for inappropriate behavior.

If I've arranged a meeting in my New York office with a well-known billionaire and he strolls in dressed in running shorts and eating an ice cream cone, I might think that's strange. But I'd probably keep that thought to myself. He's a billionaire. He has the track record and credibility to get away with it. But if one of our junior executives tried the same stunt during business hours, I'd seriously question his judgment.

A few years ago, when we were working with the organizers of the America's Cup, one of our senior executives went to a meeting with the directors of the San Diego Yacht Club wearing jeans and tennis shoes, assuming that everybody in California dressed that casually. All the directors wore suits and ties. If he was America's Cup champion Dennis Conner, I suppose he could have gotten away with that attire. But he wasn't and consequently made a bad impression.

These wrong assumptions become particularly problematic in the area of perks and privileges. Your top performers at some point have earned certain perks—the first-class travel, the luxury suites, the country club memberships, the corner office, the extra secretary, etc. They've paid their dues in terms of time, effort, and results. A lot of people misjudge how much dues they've paid and feel entitled to these same privileges. And so they spend company resources in a manner totally at odds with their standing in the company.

This same miscalculation applies to opinions. People will often overestimate the value of their opinions or even if anyone wants to hear them. Not long ago I had an internal meeting with some senior and junior executives to discuss an upcoming event. The discussion became heated as the senior people weighed in with strong opinions about who should and shouldn't participate in the event. There's nothing wrong with that. These were people I've worked with for years. I expect them to challenge me and speak their mind. At some point one of the junior executives decided to join the fray and started offering his opinions. He was mimicking his superiors, even though he knew very little about the subject. Finally, I turned to him and said, "This year you listen. Next year you get to talk."

In a nutshell, that may be the only way to deal with people who assume they can play by the superstar's rules. Make them prove they deserve the privilege. Until then, tell them they have to wait.

• • •
THE McCORMACK RULES

- There is no quicker way to gauge a company's efficiency than by counting how many rings it takes for your call to get through.

- First-rate management tends to deliver first-rate results.

- If you know a rival company is on its way down, you can often pick up its most valuable pieces at distress sale prices.

- All investments are risky. Admitting that to yourself is the first step in reducing the risk.

- Managers who cannot maintain a sense of impending crisis within their organization will probably be facing real crises sooner than they imagine.

- No matter what business you're in, the first employee should be a salesperson.

- You can't call yourself an international company if you don't have a lot of international accents running through it.

- Recessions are the best times for much-needed austerity measures, because no one in their right mind can argue with you.

- If you ever considered paring down your payroll, a recession will pinpoint where you should start.

- Most managers treat bad news the same way they treat criticism. They either deny it or demean it. Rarely do they accept it or deal with it. Even more rarely do they demand it.

- The bigger the disaster, the calmer you must be.

- The most crucial similarity between criticism and bad news is that you have to demand it to get it. And you have to demand it sooner rather than later. Bad news delayed or delivered slowly is bad news squared.

- If you want to keep your top performers happy, give them first crack at the hot emerging areas in your business.

CHAPTER 10

What's Your
Managing IQ?

N ow let's see what you've learned. The following hypo-
theticals can stump even the most experienced managers.

PRETENDING THE GLASS IS HALF
FULL, NOT HALF EMPTY

Q: Your division has just suffered two stinging customer defections. The losses have not only hit your bottom line (and
dropped you from the top spot among the company's line divisions) but badly damaged morale. Several key employees
have offered to resign (you declined their offer). How do you
rebuild the division's confidence after a setback?

A: Every leader has some sort of mental gymnastics routine for coping with defeat, rejection, or loss. The one element these routines have in common is a healthy dose of denial. If a customer defection is crippling your staff, you probably need a little more denial in your life.

That doesn't mean you should pretend the customer defections never happened. You know they happened. The proof is there on your bottom line.

But it's completely unrealistic for you to think that the losses *shouldn't* have happened. After all, what business holds on to 100 percent of its customers in perpetuity? In other words, you have to find a way to *deny*—to yourself if not the outside world—that these defections signify something more than business as usual. They don't mean you're bad or incompetent or unworthy of staying in business. They simply come with the territory.

I've never had a hard time making that mental adjustment. Whenever we've lost a client, I've always made a concerted effort to sign up a new client as soon as possible. There's a business reason for this, of course: In a personal services business, where you don't always have the time or staff to take on a new client, the loss of a client frees you up to take on another. There's also a psychological reason: You're less likely to dwell on a lost client if you're forced to focus on a newly acquired one.

In other words, I count my gains, not my losses. I suggest you do the same.

It helps, of course, if you have some gains to count. So your first step should be an aggressive campaign to replace the two precious customers you lost. Your second step should be a little internal spin control. You may not sound convincing telling the outside world, "The clients did-n't quit; we fired them." But a variation on that message may find welcome ears internally. Your people need to hear you say that the glass is half full, not half empty.

BREAKING DOWN WALLS
BETWEEN FACTIONS

Q: In the last three months in your new job, you have replaced forty-five employees in your ninety-person department. That's what you were brought in to do: inject new blood into the or-ganization. Your problem is dealing with the survivors, the peo-ple you've kept. They're good, but many of them are so differ-ent from the new recruits that it seems you have unintentionally segmented the department into old guard and new guard. How do you break down the wall between the two factions?

A: Organizational changes don't happen by decree. They don't happen overnight. And they don't happen because of one grand, sweeping gesture (even when it is a massive half-the-staff housecleaning like yours). The most lasting changes hap-pen in waves, carefully calibrated, designed, and timed.

If you've turned over half the staff, you're definitely past the first wave. The second wave requires you to decide what to do with the people you've kept.

The easiest way to get the veterans to shed their "old guard" thinking is to give them new assignments. They'll be so busy learning the new job, they won't get a chance to say, "This is how we always did it."

261

This happened a few years back to an editor I know who was hired to rebuild a major city newspaper. He inherited a tired, entrenched newsroom of editors and reporters. After sorting out the deadwood and raiding other papers for talent, his newsroom was still largely "old guard." He knew this group had talent, but he didn't need them to cover their beats the way they always did. So he simply reassigned as many of them as possible to totally new beats. Political writers went to the business section. Metro editors switched to state and national desks. Wherever possible, the grizzled veterans were forced to work on equal footing with new hires. The risk was that the new guard would pick up the veterans' bad habits. The actual payoff was that they didn't.

Of course, it helped that my friend made these radical changes quietly and slowly, so that very few people noticed what he was doing.

If you want to bring your two factions together, first change the old guard's jobs. By doing so, you change the makeup of their peer group, the colleagues they work with daily. In doing that, you can't help but change their habits and attitudes.

Old dogs will learn new tricks if new dogs are doing the teaching.

WHEN THE CREW JUMPS SHIP

Q: Three of your most promising executives recently jumped shipped to an archrival. It started with one executive, who then lured two of his colleagues away. How do you stop the competition from poaching your executive pool? More important, what can you do to stop the one that got away from taking more with him?

A: At our company, I like to say we've never lost anyone we didn't want to lose. To a large degree that's true. Certainly people have left whose departure caused us some grief, but at the senior management level our ranks have been incredibly stable.

The irony is that we've tried the standard tactics to combat talent raids—asking executives to sign non-compete agreements and instituting a "golden handcuffs" compensation policy (staggering part of their compensation over several years and paying it out only as long as they're with us). But I'm not convinced that's what keeps people on board.

At best, the non-compete agreement tends to prevent surprise or hostile departures; it forces an executive to leave amicably or risk legal retaliation. The staggered payout merely makes a departure more expensive—either for the departing executive or for his new company if he was smart enough to negotiate a payout for any lost income. (It eases some of the pain to know one of my competitors is paying a former executive money that we once owed to that executive.) But I don't believe you can keep people against their will. If they really want to go, it's usually best to let them go with your blessing.

The best approach is to focus on stopping the one that got away from raiding his former home. That's where the real damage is done. You can lose an entire department of people if they go along with a charismatic leader. The best tactic is prevention: Tie up as much of your talented people's compensation—their bonuses, their perks, their special pension funds, etc.—as possible to a promise that they won't hire from your ranks. You can't always stop people from leaving, but you can make it painful for them to ask others to follow.

SPARE A MINUTE, NOT AN HOUR

Q: Your work has been suffering because of constant inter-ruptions. If it isn't a ringing phone, then it's subordinates out-side your closed door, knocking and asking, "Do you have a minute?" How do you cut down the interruptions?

A: Hint: When subordinates ask if you have a minute to spare, do you ever say "no"?

The problem with interruptions is not so much that they can derail your train of thought or destroy your schedule or make you forget your priorities (although these are all bad) but rather that they tend to snowball. Allow one interruption and everyone else thinks it's their privilege, too. People who don't get interrupted are people who don't tolerate interruptions.

The interesting thing about interruptions is that they increase rather than decrease as you move up the corporate ladder.

You'd think, for example, that CEOs are the least inter-ruptible people in an organization. They have the heaviest agendas, the tightest schedules, the fewest minutes to spare, and the most pressure on them. They don't have time for interruptions.

Not true. The best CEOs know that attending to the lit-tle blips and burps in their carefully constructed day is perhaps the most important part of their job. And so, early on in their careers they learn to schedule interruptions into their day. They learn to say, "I'll get back to you," and mean it.

I have two open-ended periods in my business day—usually from 11 to noon in the morning and from 5 to 6 o'clock at the end of the day. I pour all the day's interruptions—the phone calls I refused to take and promised to return, the subordinates with "pressing" problems that can hold for a few more hours—into these two hours. I may respond to interruptions at my convenience but no one can call me unresponsive.

Choosing Between Two Equal Candidates

Q: Two of your best subordinates have tossed their hats into the ring for a new management position. They're both entitled to the promotion, but only one will get it. It's your call. How do you "position" your decision so the "loser" doesn't feel he lost?

A: It would be great if you could take the two candidates' qualifications, feed them into a computer, and let the computer spit out an objective, perfectly reasoned and quantified decision. But that's not going to happen. Emotion and intuition will, in some measure, dictate your choice. That's what makes the loser feel bitter—that his or her career rides on a decision that is so *arbitrary*.

Having some clear criteria for who gets the promotion can minimize this. The more criteria you have, the less arbitrary the decision seems. For example, here are four popular criteria for choosing between people up for a promotion.

1. Which of the candidates can you least afford to lose? This is the classic risk-reward decision. You don't promote someone because of the good they will do in the new job, but rather to avoid the fallout from their departure when they are passed over. You are not creating a brilliant solution. You are merely containing some short-term damage. The fallacy here is that the promotion doesn't always go to the best person for the job but rather the one who is (a) most valuable to you in their current position (and perhaps should remain in that position) or (b) most willing to abandon you if you don't hand the promotion to them. In effect, you are responding to a real or imagined threat. That's not always good decision making, and it's hardly a reason that will soothe the loser. How would you like to hear that you are expendable and your competition isn't?

2. Who has the best track record? This is the most objective (and hence, least arbitrary) criterion. You promote your top salesperson, your most creative designer, your winningest dealmaker as a reward for past performance. The assumption is that these people will repeat that performance in the new spot. The fallacy here is that the skills that make someone excel at Job A are not always transferable to Job B. We've all seen superb salespeople, designers, and dealmakers flounder when they have been promoted into management slots. They (and the company) would have been better off if they had stuck to selling, designing, and dealmaking. This is the safest, most logical criterion for promoting people. It is tough to dispute. It is least likely to offend the loser in a race for a promotion. But it is also the reason the Peter Principle was invented.

3. Who will offend the fewest people? This turns the promotion into a popularity contest. You canvass your employees for their opinion about who they want to see in the spot. The big problem here, of course, is that you are turning your responsibility into a group decision. I don't see how the loser in this scenario will enjoy the vote or respect you for counting the ballots.

4. Who do you think can do the job? This is where decision making turns into art rather than science. You take a bunch of hard-to-quantify factors, mix them up, and play your best hunch. This is inherently arbitrary, but you can make the contest a little more fair by letting the candidates make their case in front of you. If you give each of them a chance to argue on their own behalf, they're less likely to blame you for the decision. The truth is, the losers will only have themselves to blame.

KEEPING FRIENDS CLOSE,
ENEMIES CLOSER

Q: You are the head of a rapidly growing company, answerable only to the chairman of the board and two foreign investors. A young employee whom you hired four months ago recently sent a letter to the chairman itemizing what he felt were your managerial deficiencies. The chairman is a close friend of yours and showed you the letter, telling you to deal with it as you saw fit. You confront the employee about the letter. He explains it away as a knee-jerk overreaction to a group meeting that didn't go his way. This doesn't explain the fact that he had discussed the letter with colleagues before he sent it to the chairman. You want to treat this able employee as if the incident never happened, but you cannot accept that he betrayed you. How do you deal with a worthy employee who has lost your trust?

A: You don't need to read Machiavelli's *The Prince* to handle such an egregious act of betrayal. My first inclination would be to dismiss him—for ignorance, not disloyalty. Going around you to the chairman in writing *and* thinking that you would never get wind of it is a sign of gross stupidity. As a general rule, you should never say, and certainly never write, anything about an associate, customer, or client that you wouldn't want them to hear—because they always will. In breaking that rule, your subordinate displayed a form of stupidity that I would just as soon keep out of my company.

My second inclination would be to put him on probation. Tell him that he made a mistake, that it's pointless to pretend it didn't happen (because it did happen), and give him a fixed amount of time to win back your trust. Given your bitter feelings, there's no way you can salvage this otherwise able employee. Why not force him to salvage himself?

My third inclination—and this *would* be Machiavellian—would be to reassign him to an area where he must work closely with you. This follows the Sicilian maxim: "Keep your friends close and your enemies closer." It also turns the tables on a potential foe by forcing him to work with you, acknowledge your authority, and possibly get to know you better. He may see that you are not as managerially deficient as he thinks and come to respect you more. Stranger things have happened.

You Can't Delegate Bad News

Q: As president of a company with 200 employees, you are blessed with a phenomenal executive assistant. She is so good you can even delegate to her much of the everyday communications between you and your managers. Although this delegating procedure saves precious time, you didn't count on the resentment it generates. Apparently your executives don't like hearing your decrees from your assistant. Even though she is more senior than many of them in terms of longevity and (in truth) compensation, they regard her as a secretary, someone who isn't worthy of conveying "life and death" messages to them. How do you get them to show her more respect?

A: It depends on the kinds of messages you're sending through her. If you're delegating a disproportionate amount of negative or unpleasant messages to her—and saving most of the "good news" conversations for yourself—you have only yourself to blame for how others regard her. You've made her your hatchet man. People see her coming and know that bad news will surely follow. Is it any wonder they resent her?

You're also not doing yourself any favors. Using her as the "heavy" may strike some people as spineless.

The one thing you can't delegate is bad news. You have to deliver that yourself. No matter how unpleasant the fallout, people will always respect you more, not less, for delivering bad news firsthand.

A few years ago I went out of my way to set up a meeting for a client with someone the client had always expressed a keen desire to talk to. The client's secretary called me back to say the client was neither available nor interested in such a meeting anymore. I could accept the fact that circumstances change and the client's interest in talking to this person had waned. What I couldn't accept was that the client didn't call me himself after I had extended myself on his behalf. At the least he owed me an explanation. Conversely, if his secretary called me to accept the meeting, I wouldn't have minded at all.

Two messages. One method. Two different results. That's the good news/bad news dichotomy in a nutshell.

If you want the troops to respect your assistant, give her more positive messages to deliver on your behalf. Think about it. Whom would you rather deal with? The person who's always telling you, "No, the boss turned down your proposal" or the person who's saying, "Your budget increase was approved"? Believe me, after hearing a few positive sounds from your assistant, they'll quickly regard her as a positive force at the company.

SOUND THE ALARM WHEN CUTTING COSTS

Q: Expenses are running out of control in several of your divisions. How do you contain costs without alarming the troops?

A: Alarming the troops is precisely what you should be doing! How else are they going to believe that there is a crisis?

The life cycle of nearly every company is a continuum of expansion and contraction. In the expansion mode, everything is great. The company is profitable and willing to invest in the future. In this optimistic environment, employees

270

can get reckless about costs. They'll buy new office equipment, add staff, travel and entertain more aggressively. It's
usually a gradual process. For example, one executive acquires
new office furniture. His peers see this and feel they're entitled to the same privilege. Before long this snowballs into a
company-wide redecoration.

That's when you have to shift into contraction mode.
Fast.

Separate all expenses into "must have" and "nice to have."
And eliminate all of the latter. You'll be surprised how resourceful your employees can be once you have reordered
their priorities.

MONITORING SALARIES LIKE
AN INVESTMENT

Q: During the past three years, your company has grown from
a handful of employees to more than a hundred. One conse-
quence of this rapid growth is that your compensation structure
is a mess. It has no rhyme or reason. You've personally negotiated salary with every new employee. Some people got good
deals for themselves; others came at bargain rates. As a result,
you have some people who earn twice as much as their peers,
with no appreciable difference in their responsibilities, performance, or rank. Your banker thinks this is a recipe for disaster. Eventually, the "bargain rate" employees will revolt—
which could be costly. This banker suggests that a salary grading
system similar to his bank's or the government's would be more
equitable. Do you?

A: This is an interesting puzzle because it assumes that (a) the people who negotiated big salaries for themselves are over-paid, (b) the "bargain" employees are underpaid, and (c) some-where in between is a fair compensation base for the company.

In other words, if the high end of your compensation structure is, say, $100,000 and the low end is $50,000, your problems would be solved if you adjusted everyone's salary to a base of $75,000. That wouldn't cost you any money and it would inject some fairness into your compensation policy.

The big problem here, of course, is that it's undoable. You cannot cut people's salaries without serious consequences.

Another problem—and this is my big gripe with salary grades—is that you are dealing with people here, not posi-tions. Salary grades may work in large, static organizations, such as government bureaucracies, where you hire and pay people for filling specific posts. Grading assumes that people are interchangeable parts. If they prove to be exceptional, you promote them to a higher post. At some point they peak—and either remain in place, retire, or move into the more dy-namic private sector. Either way, an exceptional person has been underutilized.

That static system doesn't apply to your company, which is growing so rapidly. If you're hiring talented people in a dy-namic company, their responsibilities should be changing every six to twelve months. Their jobs can't be defined (or confined) within the limits of a graded position.

Salary grades are not the answer here. They certainly don't eliminate the inequity you're talking about—since there will always be exceptional people at a specific grade who think they are carrying more weight than their less-than-exceptional peers.

Your banker is wrong. You're compensating your people as fairly as can be expected. You're always going to have some people who are overpaid and others who are underpaid. In the long run it balances out. The overpaid people tend to be held to higher standards; if they don't deliver on the raised expectations, they eventually get weeded out. If the underpaid people surprise you with their exceptional performance, they're usually rewarded with a pay increase.

It's a fluid, self-correcting process not unlike the stock market. In the stock market, you will always have some companies whose shares are overvalued and some that are undervalued. That's because there are a lot of vague, subjective criteria that go into establishing share price.

It's just as fuzzy with compensation, where you probably pay people in part based on your opinion of their experience (past earnings), salary history (market value), and their growth potential (projected earnings). Your situation is no different from that of an investor. You've "bought high" with some employees and "low" with others. Your task is to monitor your investments closely and get rid of the ones that are overpriced and invest some more in the ones that are underpriced. You won't solve this problem with salary grades.

THE KEY TO SHORTER MEETINGS

Q: You spend 60 percent of your time in internal meetings, in part because virtually all your meetings run longer than scheduled. You think that's an unhealthy percentage. How do you make your meetings shorter?

A: It's hard to say what a healthy percentage of time spent in meetings is. It depends on your job. I know some effective executives who spend nearly all their time in internal meetings. It's their job to find out what's going on, to bring people together, and to make things happen. But if you spent 30 percent of your time in meetings two years ago and felt you were accomplishing more, then 60 percent is unhealthy.

To shorten meetings, you might consider what the former American Secretary of State James Baker did on taking over President George Bush's presidential campaign in 1992. One of Baker's first decrees as the new chief of staff was to *limit all meetings to a single subject*. It obeys what staffers called "Baker's First Law of Coherence." Attendees gathered to solve a single problem are less likely to launch into little speeches.

REPLACING YOURSELF WITH SOMEONE BETTER, NOT WORSE

Q: Your boss tells you that a big reason you haven't been promoted is that he loves the job you're doing. Unfortunately, hearing him say, "I can't afford to lose you" is small comfort to your career. How do you change the boss's mind?

A: Hint: Have you found your replacement?

Bosses want solutions, not problems. Right now in your boss's mind your "promotion" is really your "departure." That's a problem. If you found someone to take your place, you would be creating a solution. That's an offer no boss can refuse.

One caveat: Be sure that your replacement is as good if not better than you. Don't let your ego get in the way. It will only come back to haunt you.

In the mid-1980s, when my New York secretary wanted to move to another part of the company, I agreed but insisted that she find her replacement first. We went through three secretaries in six months before it dawned on me that she would never hire someone as efficient as she was. Consciously or not, she was providing me with mediocrities. Perhaps she thought that by doing so her value would increase in my eyes. Actually, the opposite was true.

RESOLVING A DISPUTE LIKE SOLOMON

Q: One of your people insists you choose between her and a colleague she claims is obstructing her. You'd prefer to keep them both. How do you resolve a dispute between two employees?

A: Before you do anything, determine if what she claims is, in fact, true. Force her to repeat her charges to her colleague's face. It's the most potent truth serum. It might even force her to soften her position.

Even if she's telling the truth, don't let her force you into the role of judge and jury. You can certainly give both of them a fair hearing, but you're under no obligation to render a verdict (especially not when it might alienate or destroy one of them).

As the boss, you're better off giving them instructions (*i.e.*, what to do) rather than opinions (*i.e.*, what you think).

Thus, you should bring them together, insist that they sort it out soon, and then leave the room.

If these duelists are worth hanging on to, they will find a way to follow your instructions to the letter.

To Share or Not to Share
Numbers

Q: You and your partner are philosophically at odds about how free you should be with information at your company. Your partner thinks you should reveal as little of the "numbers" to staff as possible. He's afraid that the data will somehow get out to your competition and be used against you. You think the more you tell your people, the less suspicious they are and the more able they are to make informed judgments. Which is the right approach?

A: It depends on what kind of business you're in. If you're a manufacturer and one of your competitive advantages is a low-cost deal you've negotiated with a supplier in Hong Kong, I'd be careful about how widely I would want the terms of that arrangement disseminated through the company. You don't want everyone to know that—because a competitor could simply hire away an employee and learn one of your "trade secrets." If you restrict that sort of information to a select group of executives, the information is less likely to get out. If it does, it will cost the competition dearly because they will have to hire a senior executive to access it.

In other words, I would be cautious with proprietary information that the competition could actually act on.

Having said that, however, I think people tend to overestimate how valuable or how secret their so-called corporate secrets are. For example, in our business of creating and marketing sports events, we have developed certain areas of expertise in generating revenue (*e.g.*, selling television rights internationally) and reducing operating costs (*e.g.*, bartering aggressively) that make the event business profitable for us. We could show our competitors step-by-step how we implement an event—and we frequently have in sports marketing seminars. But that doesn't mean they can compete with us. Our "trade secrets" are useless unless our competitors can execute them with our discipline for maximizing revenue and our tenacity at minimizing costs. Quite often, they can't. Execution, not information, is our edge.

I also think people overestimate the value of financial information. If your company is publicly traded, theoretically you are an open book. The whole world sees your profit-and-loss statement. Yet that doesn't necessarily make you more vulnerable to attack from competitors. In fact, in a way, it is liberating. If everyone knows a piece of information, how unique and valuable can it be?

In this case I go along with the partner who wants to share information. When management hides vital numbers from employees, the employees often end up making wild assumptions that can damage the business.

For example, when employees are kept in the dark about a company's income and outgo, they tend to get suspicious about the company's riches. They often draw unrealistic conclusions about how much the bosses are raking in. From there, it's not too great a leap for people to exaggerate how much money the company has to spend on compensation, perks, and travel and entertainment. Sharing financial information can give employees a valuable dose of reality and make them appreciate the true costs of staying in business.

It's Better to Promote Quickly Rather Than Slowly

Q: You've lost two good people in the last month because they didn't feel you were promoting people fast enough. Is it time to change your policy?

A: The short answer is yes.

I've always thought it's better to promote a little too quickly rather than too slowly. And your problem is the strongest argument for that viewpoint. The big plus in promoting quickly is that it creates a grateful (and slightly nervous) employee who will work even harder to justify your confidence in him or her. The big minus in promoting slowly is that the good people leave you before you ever get the chance to reward them.

Sharing the Pain of Downsizing

Q: You are going through a periodic downsizing at your company. Should you dictate across-the-board cuts to all departments or should you let the department heads handle it on their own?

A: At the risk of waffling, I don't think it's an either/or proposition. There's a middle ground between telling people what to do and letting them know what you had in mind.

I always think it's wiser to make the people who will bear the brunt of the cost cutting not only share the pain but share in the decision. If you tell a department head to cut $250,000 from his budget, he probably has a better idea of how and where to cut than you do. He knows which employees are carrying their weight and which ones aren't. He knows which expenditures are "nice to have" and which are "must have."

My advice: Give the department heads a target number but let them decide how to reach that number. Then make them justify it to you and your directors.

WHEN EMPLOYEES GIVE YOU ONLY HALF THE PICTURE

Q: You have a gnawing suspicion that your subordinates are not being totally candid with you. They're holding back or putting a positive spin on some of the bad news that you really need to know. How do you let employees know that they can tell you anything without fear of retribution?

A: You can certainly tell employees that you expect them to be straight with you. But that's meaningless if you don't show them day in and day out that you can accept the unvarnished truth gracefully.

Many managers have a "kill the messenger" complex. They overreact to bad news—either out of immaturity or lack of self-control or even a misguided notion that displaying their anger will somehow have a telling effect on their subordinates.

They'd be better off underreacting.

In a way, I almost brace myself to hear bad news by adopting a mask of serenity. It has a calming effect on the worried messenger and goes a long way to ensuring that he or she will continue to tell me the full truth in the future. It certainly makes more sense than blowing up at them.

I also realize that eliciting the truth from people is like pulling teeth. If an employee is reluctant to tell me straight out that a project is not meeting expectations, I'll tell him straight out, "I don't care how much money we're losing. Just tell me so I have an idea what we'll need to fix it." Thus reassured, the employee invariably opens up.

MAKING SOMEONE ELSE'S DECISION YOUR OWN

Q: You run the most profitable division of a private company. The owner likes the job you're doing, even though he often undermines your authority. Most recently, he hired two executives (a husband-wife team) without telling you. You learned it from the owner's daughter, who also works for you, the day before the duo came on board. Although you can use the extra manpower, you're not thrilled with his method. Your big worry is that because the owner hired this duo, they will always feel they report to the owner, not you. How do you correct this situation and re-establish your authority?

A: First, let's make one thing clear: The owner screwed up.

He should have included you in the hiring decision— not because it's the polite thing to do, or it spares your feelings, or it props up your authority, but because it's the only way to make the decision work. Subordinates tend to support decisions they participate in and sabotage (unconsciously or otherwise) those they are excluded from.

Now that we've established that you are in the right, what do you do?

You can complain to the boss to show him the error of his ways. (Don't expect to change him.)

You can undermine the decision and help it fail. (Don't expect his gratitude.)

Or you can co-opt the decision and make it your own. Since you agree with the move, this shouldn't be hard to do. You should immediately take the new hirees under your wing. Give them assignments. Set their budgets, priorities, and re-porting procedures. Do this before your boss does, and he'll probably thank you for it.

LET'S SWAP SECRETARIES

Q: Your longtime secretary says she's "burned out" in her job. The catch is that she's not threatening you with this. She's not thinking of quitting or pursuing a promotion. She's happy where she is. How do you recharge her batteries?

A: You should consider swapping secretaries with a colleague in a different department or office or city or country.

A few years ago I came up with the idea of swapping my London and New York secretaries for three months. I thought it would be good for each of them to actually see the faces of all the people they had been communicating with for years across the Atlantic. It would teach them how office personnel and procedures differ in each country, which in turn would help them deal with that office more effectively when they returned. They might pick up a few operational ideas during their stay that could work back home—or they might bring some good ideas with them. Also, there was the perk element. Three months in New York or London is a nice living experience to some people.

Not everyone, of course, has the type of business that can accommodate employee swaps between New York and London. But the slightest change of scene—even to the department next door—will have an impact and can shake any employee's lethargy.

Managing by the Markdown Theory

Q: You think you've made a hiring mistake with your new assistant. But you feel you should give him at least several weeks to prove you wrong. What is an appropriate period of time for giving new hires the benefit of the doubt?

A: Time has nothing to do with it. Sometimes you can tell that a new person is totally wrong for your company within twenty-four hours. (Quite often, the new person realizes this, too.) Sometimes it takes several years before you know.

What you really have to gauge is why your new assistant displeases you and whether that is likely to change in the near future.

The owner of a chain of discount stores once said, "If a subordinate disappoints you once, discount his credibility by 10 percent. If he disappoints a second time, 30 percent. If he does it a third time, sell out at any price."

This "markdown theory of management" may not apply in every situation, but it's a useful guideline once you have your suspicions about a new hire.

Also, as a matter of fairness, be sure to tell your new assistant that he is, in effect, on "probation." If that doesn't motivate him to meet your standards of performance, nothing will.

Index
